Language and Connection
in Psychotherapy

Language and Connection in Psychotherapy

Words Matter

Mary Davis, MD

JASON ARONSON
Lanham • Boulder • New York • Toronto • Plymouth, UK

Published by Jason Aronson
A wholly owned subsidiary of The Rowman & Littlefield Publishing Group, Inc.
4501 Forbes Boulevard, Suite 200, Lanham, Maryland 20706
www.rowman.com

10 Thornbury Road, Plymouth PL6 7PP, United Kingdom

British Library Cataloguing in Publication Information Available

Library of Congress Cataloging-in-Publication Data

Davis, Mary, 1949-
Language and connection in psychotherapy : words matter / Mary Davis.
p. cm.
Includes bibliographical references and index.
ISBN 978-0-7657-0873-1 (cloth : alk. paper) -- ISBN 978-0-7657-0874-8 (electronic)
1. Psychotherapist and patient. 2. Psychotherapy--Language. I. Title.
RC480.8.D37 2013
616.89'14--dc23
2012034844

™
The paper used in this publication meets the minimum requirements of American National Standard for Information Sciences Permanence of Paper for Printed Library Materials, ANSI/NISO Z39.48-1992.

Printed in the United States of America

Contents

Acknowledgments

When I read acknowledgments in other books, I always wonder what the people named did to merit recognition. I know what the people who helped me did, and I know this is a better book because of their support and encouragement.

My sisters, Patricia Davis and Cynthia Davis, kindly agreed to be my primary readers. Because of their comments and other conversations with them, I reorganized the book at least twice, improving it over time. Our mutual love of scholarship, reading, writing, and words is learned from our parents.

I met Cressida Forester online when I wrote to ask permission to quote her. As we began corresponding about what I intended, her interest and enthusiasm greatly encouraged me and raised new questions for me to consider.

Joan Turkus is a friend and colleague, who shares in my struggle to write clearly and concisely. I met her through the New Directions Psychoanalytic Writing Program at the Washington Center for Psychoanalysis, which enhanced my professional life and my writing skills.

M. Hossein Etezady, a colleague and friend, encouraged me to write, offered me opportunities to do so, and often made apparently casual remarks that opened new ways of thinking about and understanding my patients and my writing.

And finally, of course, my patients have enriched me immeasurably, both in showing what I've tried to explain here and in allowing me to be a part of their lives.

Introduction

I spend my days using words and language to help people heal—using the "talking cure." Words are the tools I use to communicate with and help my patients. The "data" I use in my work, akin to the physical examination by the internist or the pediatrician, are the words and behaviors of my patients. As I listen to what my patients say, and observe their behavior with me and with others, I construct theories about how to understand the suffering that brings them to my office.

Most often words and language suffice for this work, but sometimes words are not enough. This book is about what we can do, then, in therapy and in life. Because words often are enough, and because they do matter, it is also about the many ways words and what we do with them shape our lives, and how we communicate (or not) with them. I begin with the clinical perspective and how these issues affect my patients. I then look at what clinical experience teaches us about the things language can and cannot do in daily life.

People come to see me for psychiatric and psychoanalytic treatment because they are unhappy or because they cannot do what they want in their lives. They may be chronically sad or angry; they may have noticed uncomfortable behavioral patterns, such as losing their temper easily and "flipping out"; they may have relational problems, such as multiple failed marriages. Sometimes they have cognitive difficulties, such as the inability to think clearly or to concentrate because of intrusive thoughts or feelings; or perceptual problems, such as seeing or hearing things others do not see or hear. When these patients appear in my office, I use language to gather information about their suffering, to offer a possible treatment, to begin the process of helping them. I develop relationships with my patients which, like all relationships, are carried both by language and by the nonverbal elements of

1

communication. With experience, I have developed a sense for how the therapeutic relationship progresses and for how a particular psychotherapeutic encounter is likely to proceed when it is going well. And then, without warning, I encounter a situation where the ways in which I know to help don't work. Such situations stimulated the thoughts in this book.

In chapter 1, Kay is one of the people for whom words were not enough. For her, listening and talking in the usual ways did not carry healing. In her treatment, we recognized a disruption of the emotional connections of words to her inner experience. This made her unable to use words to convey her sense of self even to herself. This chapter describes how we worked around, with, and through that disruption to help Kay move towards recognizing and expressing herself.

Kay gave me permission to use her material, as did Barbara, in chapter 3. Although I was not able to obtain similar permission from every patient mentioned, because I could not locate some of them, all material about patients is disguised to prevent the identification of the actual individuals.

We know nonverbal modes of communication can be helpful. There are large groups of professionals who use body therapy, play therapy, art therapy, dance therapy, music therapy, and other nonverbal modes of therapy to help wounded people heal. In traditional psychotherapy with adult patients, nonverbal modes of communication supplement language, as we notice body posture or anxious mannerisms. Sometimes even a change in dress, more or less casual than we are accustomed to, offers information about the state of our relationship with our patients. With Kay I learned nonverbal modes of communication—for her, visual art—can be *more* important and *more* helpful than talking and words.

As I learned and thought about these issues with Kay, I thought about other patients from my years of practice. Sue, in chapter 2, is a young girl who could not use language to connect with others because of a profound disturbance that affected her ability to deal effectively with the world around her. In her year of work with me, building on previous years with other therapists, she learned to think and, thus, to talk about her inner experience in ways new to her. When Sue was unable to think about her inner experience, she was unable to talk to others in ways that fostered positive connections. Her newfound ability to think about herself allowed a major shift in her development, as it opened new possibilities for relating to others and for functioning in the world.

In thinking about Kay and Sue, my ideas about language and communication, and how they serve in daily functioning, expanded dramatically. I recognized the ways language can *impede* functioning, including within psychotherapy or psychoanalysis. It serves to separate us from others at times, as well as to connect us with others. Chapters 3 and 4 deal with some of the ways language brings us closer to others, as well as separates us from them.

It is possible to convey the same information in multiple ways, but the way in which we say it offers information about ourselves, about our relationship to the listener, and about what we hope for from the conversation. The *way* one speaks—slowly or fast, in complete sentences or fragmented phrases, using a dialect unfamiliar to the listener, using jargon or verbal shortcuts—creates a particular level of distance or intimacy between the people listening and talking, a relational distance of sorts. In chapter 3, I explore some of the ways the *form* of our language can determine the interpersonal *function* of the communication.

In chapter 4, I look at the different "languages" we use: the different ways we speak with family, with close friends, with business associates, and how those different languages help to determine the nature of our relationships. I also discuss the dyadic nature of verbal communication, how the nature of the communication is determined not only by what is said, but by the nature of the listener and his or her life experience and predispositions.

In the first half of the book, then, I discuss why and how these issues matter to us, why it is important to think, talk, and write about them. In chapter 5, I describe the generally expected path of language acquisition, so we can begin to understand some of what has gone wrong when we meet an adult whose verbal communicative patterns are unexpected, when we find words are not enough for our task. As I describe the developmental line of language acquisition, I note along the way points where we can see very early versions of capacities we take for granted in adults.

In this chapter, and indeed throughout the book, I use "he" and "she" interchangeably to indicate babies and other individuals of either gender. I also use "mother" as shorthand referring to the baby's primary nurturing figure. We should remember, however, not all caretakers are mothers or even women, and babies are girls as well as boys.

Chapter 6 looks at some of the ways the expected developmental path may diverge, as in deaf children of hearing adults or hearing children of deaf parents. I consider children with Asperger's disorder, who are sometimes described as having intact language. For these children, even when the semantics of the child's language are intact, the pragmatics—the ways one uses language to relate to others—are distorted. I also consider some of the ways early development teaches children to use language to *hide* themselves rather than to reveal themselves to others interpersonally.

In chapter 7, we consider the ways our language, both receptive (how we hear what others say) and expressive (how we say what we mean), reflects our past experience. The world in which we learned to speak and to listen to others affects, greatly, how we understand their words, as well as what words we use to describe our own lives. For instance, "father" means something very different to me than it would to someone whose father died in his infancy, or whose father was abusive. Events in later life add their own emotional meanings to words, as the memories that accompany words for life events add themselves to the stream of thoughts about each word. People with a history of trauma provide a clear way to examine these issues. For these people, the experiences that connect words with memory are so intense and overwhelming that the ways in which they use the words that evoke the memories are noticeably different. In psychotherapeutic situations, they often react to our verbal interactions in surprising ways. For instance, a patient who has never felt safe may not grasp the concept of a safe place, because there is no such thing. Traumatized individuals may be more likely to use language to hide themselves and their emotional reactions to us, in fear of further abuse. For some, certain words can trigger flashbacks, intrusive memories of the trauma. Patterns of not knowing or of distorting the meanings of words disrupt relationships, including the relationship that supports and contains the therapy. Trauma patients are unlikely to find relief from treatment until the distortions of language, and of relationships that rely on language, are recognized and understood. Until they are able to speak about the unspeakable things that happened to them, they continue to suffer.

These situations teach us language is much more than grammar and syntax. It is alive, with meaning beyond the simple facts conveyed, and emotion beyond what is spoken. In chapter 8, I touch on the uses of metaphors, similes, poetry, and some of the ways language can be used to communicate what is essentially unsayable. Some things are unspeakable, because what must be spoken is too terrible to come close enough to touch. This is what we encounter in our work with traumatized individuals. Other experiences, however, are unsayable because the words we have are not adequate to convey what we want to say. I agree with Daniel Stern (1985), who suggests that because language is inadequate in communicating internal states it can create a rupture between what one says and how one feels. It can serve to separate us from our feelings, rather than connect us. We are, however, also able to use language to repair the rupture, to convey the emotions words alone constrain and constrict. Language is, in itself, inadequate in communicating emotions, but language allows us to find ways to evoke those emotions in others, so we can convey them nevertheless. In this chapter, I look at some of the ways we build bridges over the gulf between being and saying by using poetry, metaphor, similes, and other linguistic tools.

In chapter 9, I return to ask *why* words matter. What do language and words do that nothing else can? And how are we able to use the complexity of language, in our psychotherapeutic work, to help others heal? Language has an enormous capacity to connect—feelings and thoughts, individuals with each other, one's conscious cognitive self with the unconscious or preconscious emotional self. In psychotherapy, we work to find and bridge the broken connections in our patients' lives.

The psychotherapist must be a master in bridging the gap between being and saying, between experiencing and "languaging." One of the ways I understand my task as a psychotherapist is to help my patients turn behavioral language into verbal language, to find words for what they say with their actions. As we turn their behavior into words and find words for emotions, they begin to reshape themselves and their relationship to the world they inhabit. In chapter 9, I explore how that reshaping is related to our conversations together, and I raise questions for further discussion and thought.

I write both for professionals like myself—psychoanalysts and psychotherapists—and for lay persons who are interested in these issues. My thinking about these topics begins, as my interest in them did, with my clinical work and with the patients who taught me about language and its uses and misuses. At times, I write about how these considerations of language and its use shape psychotherapeutic work and the sorts of concepts we need to keep in mind as we work to connect with others, using relationship and the language of relationship to heal others. At other times, I write about how these considerations of language and its use shape everyday life. I consider how language helps us to connect to and interact with others, and some of the ways we use it to distance ourselves from others, to avoid connection, or to protect ourselves from interpersonal harm. The ways language shapes our lives are so pervasive and far-reaching they often cannot be discussed separately without some repetition, like an Escher painting, where each evolution of the figure takes us back to a previous figure.

In various places, I write about patients who taught me about language and its role in our lives. In those chapters, I try to be as alive and affectively full as my patients, so you can learn from them as I did. At other times I write about what we have learned from research and experience over the years, and often then my words are drier, more distant from feeling, speaking to technical issues about the work more than to the emotional meaning of the work.

In writing about what we know from research and experience, I wanted to write clearly, cogently, and with as little possibility for confusion as I could manage, so the unknown reader of my writing would understand me. In that persona, I use phrases like "transference," which have specific technical meanings but should be at least vaguely understandable from the context to the lay reader, and I write about the cognitive and affective components of our language.

On the other hand, the more I tried to be clear and cogent, the more specific and "factual" I became, the more I seemed to falsify the very essence of what I tried to say. Eventually I abandoned the attempt at perfect clarity, in favor of raising possibilities. Language, at its best, is alive and vibrant with emotion, it serves multiple purposes in our lives, and it cannot be pinned down. The best I am able to do is to write about some of the aspects of language in our lives, to point to ways where the different facets of the phenomenon impinge on each other, and to hint at other ways language might act in our lives. I try to help my readers piece the elephant together from separate descriptions of ear, tail, trunk, legs, and body.

It is my hope, as you read this book, that you become aware of the subtle and not-so-subtle ways the language we use reflects and affects our history, our relationships, and our way of being in the world. Words do matter. And so does what we do with them.

Chapter One

The Language of Color and Hope

We rely on language to connect with others, to reveal ourselves, to convey information, and to negotiate the tasks of everyday life. We also use it to protect ourselves, to keep secrets, and to lie. Like the air we breathe, when our language serves its function, it is transparent; we notice it most when it fails. Psychoanalysis and psychoanalytic psychotherapy rely heavily on language to carry the healing relationship and healing interactions. When language fails us in that work we may not know how to proceed.

When Kay came for treatment in her late forties, she suffered from significant depression. She seemed to find her twice-weekly therapy helpful for about eighteen months and was able to work, go to school, and maintain social relationships. In the second year of therapy, she explored a new relationship and took a break from the therapy. When she returned, she reported an increase in her depression, and we resumed twice-weekly sessions.

Fairly quickly it was clear Kay was significantly more depressed than before the break in treatment, and the treatment itself no longer proved helpful. She seemed more and more empty, emotionally, with less ability to manage her life. She began to require leaves of absence from work, due to extreme fatigue. Eventually she reached a point where she slept most of the time, and there was little in her life except therapy. She cancelled even her therapy sessions frequently, either because of severe migraines or because she was unable to get up to come in. She was so intensely depressed and despairing that we both felt almost anything that might help was worth trying, even something as extreme as electroconvulsive therapy. Various changes in medication and a trial of ECT were unhelpful.

The connection we experienced in the first part of treatment did not deepen in ways that allowed me to be helpful to Kay. I was puzzled and felt distant from her, unable to feel the mutuality of experience I knew to be the core of successful therapy. I believed we needed to create a space that felt safe for her and would allow her to come out from behind the defensive wall she created. I suggested a trial of traditional psychoanalysis, which I believed might offer a safe space. For many, it also offers a sense of timelessness that allows them to emerge at their own pace. For Kay, however, using the couch was intolerable, because not being able to see me increased her fear and despair. Generally, I am able to join with my patients fairly readily, in order to create a safe space, a "holding environment" (Winnicott, 1960, p. 590), but for Kay nothing seemed to work to invite her out of her retreat into isolation and despair.

As I cast about for ways to work with Kay more successfully, I considered using less traditional techniques to communicate about her internal life. I knew from my work with children that sometimes nonverbal—or perhaps "paraverbal"—techniques offer clues to the patient's internal life in a way words cannot, offering the chance for empathic connection. Because Kay is an artist, although she had not been able, for some years, to paint freely, I thought art might offer such an opportunity. Kay did not believe she would be able to "free associate" with her painting, or to think independently of something to paint. Despite her doubts, she was willing to try, whether out of desperation or out of a transference stance of unquestioning compliance.

We agreed on a procedure in which I told Kay what to paint—for instance "paint yourself"—and she painted it during the hour. I tried to keep my prompts open, offering only a direction without constraint. We sat side-by-side at a table as she painted and I observed. When she finished, she would put down the brush and I would say, "Tell me about that." Initially, Kay's responses to my prompts seemed not to open any doors for discussion. When I inquired about the paintings, she described, concretely, what she painted, occasionally assigning feelings to the colors, but nothing more. For instance, she might say, "It's a cave, with someone inside." I knew the cave dealt with fear, because that was the prompt, and I could guess the person inside hid in fear, but Kay could not say this until I put it into words.

Despite what I understood as Kay's inhibition of verbal associations, it quickly became clear this approach was fruitful and new things were happening in the hour. As we painted and talked, Kay and I both began to experience intense affect in the room where we had, for months before, felt only blandness and blankness. Often, neither of us could say specifically or consciously what we felt, but I felt an aliveness that Kay seemed to share. We always identified details of the picture to explore or questions to ask, where before we had felt empty with no cues to follow.

Even with the intensity of the emerging emotions, Kay could not communicate with words. At times, she sat silently with tears falling. When I inquired about the tears, she could only say, "I don't know." She was unable to recognize and express emotions or to verbalize her own inner experience, but she could paint it.

The ability to talk about emotions has its roots in early childhood, with the development of language and an ability to think about the world and about one's experience. In the early years, mother and child, together, learn language: first the baby's language, that often no one but mother understands, and then the language of the family. The capacity to label one's emotions is fed by mother's attunement, because she sees her child as a person with feelings and labels those feelings for the child. As the child learns to recognize the experience and learns the label for it—"Oh, you're sad!"—she learns to see herself as someone who has feelings. In the first months of the work with Kay and her art, we seemed to be involved in a similar process. Kay discovered she was a person with feelings that could be communicated, even if they could not be expressed in words, and then labeled as feelings.

Within myself, I struggled to find bridges to Kay's internal world. I found myself looking at each painting, which I labeled a visual metaphor, and assigning words to describe it to myself. I then was able to think about the work in a more familiar verbal way, and use my analytic self to process it. I could imagine what might be a useful question or comment, translate that thought into another visual metaphor, and ask Kay to paint that picture, as in asking her to paint what the woman hiding in the cave was afraid of. Without a translation for myself, I had no way to interact usefully with Kay about her internal world. With it, I was able to find the words she lacked and, therefore, was able to help her to explore her world. In Kay's paintings, a series of images emerged that reflected her intense and entrenched despair. Everything was black and red, and the first image of herself was a black box with a red center. Initially, she could not label the feelings, but agreed it fit when I commented my reaction was an experience of anger and despair. When we tried to explore the anger, she said only that if the box opened, things would spew out in an uncontrolled way. To me, it meant she feared she would explode and destroy herself or her world. My labeling and reflection of the emotion allowed her to recognize it, but she continued to be unable to give her own words to her emotions.

Another image that captured her sense of paralysis and despair came when I asked Kay to paint her depression: a supine body, with a heavy weight on the groin, a rope attached in such a way that she could raise the weight, but only by choking herself. We tried to explore what the weight was and what it meant, but had little success. When I commented that my own reaction was to remember her molestation at about age eight by an uncle, tears slid down her cheeks, but she neither confirmed nor denied my association.

After a few minutes, I asked Kay to tell me about the tears. She could only say, "I wish he was dead." This was the first time she was able to approach acknowledging her grief and rage at the event from which she hid for so many years. When she initially reported the molestation to me, it was in an affectless manner, ostensibly because it was "over and done with."

In one series of sessions, Kay painted representations of the various emotions: angry, afraid, sad, happy. The angry picture was a red person exploding and breaking things; the sad picture was a person sitting alone doing nothing; the frightened picture had no person in it, but was a tiny cave, in the lower corner of the canvas.

We talked about what I imagined was Kay's sense of aloneness, of hiding in the cave, and of how frightening it was to imagine coming out. She agreed, with tears, that my reaction was on target. All of the images of feelings were alone, lonely, and afraid. There was no sense of a comforting or protective presence anywhere. For Kay, her childhood had not allowed her to develop an inner sense of being a child-safe-with-mother, a memory that could be called up by mother's voice or image. She, thus, had little ability to soothe herself or to manage her emotions, so she was unable to emerge from the cave where she hid emotionally.

I asked Kay to paint herself at a time when she felt safe, and she again painted the cave where she had previously shown herself hiding. We explored it in a series of pictures early in the second year of the renewed treatment, and it emerged that the cave was safe because it kept her away from the frightening outside world, but it was also filled with her own fear and sadness. She could hear me from the cave, could imagine my presence outside, but could not always respond to me because of her fear. She could imagine coming out of the cave only if she could have a "radioactive suit to protect me from everything." Others outside the cave—including myself—were always depicted in vivid colors while Kay was in gray or black. She was able to paint pictures of herself and others, but the path to the other was always surrounded by dangerous and frightening colors, and the others were always outside the protective cave.

I talked about the paintings as if Kay and I both knew they were metaphors describing Kay's internal experience, and she seemed to accept the assumption. This was a shift from her initial sense that she had no idea where the images came from, even though she painted them.

Later in that same year, I commented that I believed Kay's loneliness (the empty cave) was how she protected herself from anger, both hers and others', and wondered what would happen if she let the anger into her central emptiness. Again, I treated the images as metaphors for her internal experience and she accepted it. She painted an amorphous image with much red and black, but also some purple, for fear. When I asked what the anger wanted, she painted a picture of herself with her eyes, mouth, nose, and ears blocked. Her anger "wanted to suffocate" her, she said, because she "made bad choices," and if she did not turn it against herself it would appear as flames out of the top of her head, driving others away but hurting only her. I asked what her anger might want if it did not want to hurt her and she painted a picture of the flames of anger opening multiple sets of eyes. When I asked her to tell me about the picture, she said clearly the anger would open the eyes of others to her own hurt and victimization.

There were several sessions when we talked about how terrible it was that no one knew about Kay's molestation; even she did not know it fully until she worked with a previous therapist and her uncle confirmed her hazy memories of his abuse. Even when people did know—her mother, for instance—they did nothing. As we talked about these issues, I believed we were finding words for the pictures, but Kay did not seem to experience any relief. I began to feel the directive interaction of the painting might lead us down the wrong path by following my thoughts, not hers, and I shared this concern with her.

We left the images of anger and went back to the safe cave, an image which was clearly Kay's and not mine. We considered the possibility that others might join her in the cave to alleviate the loneliness. She felt stuck for several days and missed some appointments because she was too depressed to come in. She talked about feeling as if she was falling into a black pit she could not escape. When she painted the pit, I was nowhere in evidence: she was clearly still all alone in her cave.

I also felt stuck and shared this with Kay. I commented on my absence from the pit, asking if she believed I was willing to be in the pit with her, with both of us working to try to get out. She was very confused by the idea, as if it was incomprehensible that I would be willing to share her pain. I asked her to paint her confusion. She painted a very powerful and distressing image, a woman in a fog made up of her confusion, anger, and fear—her eyes taped open and jangling noises at her ears.

As I considered the image of confusion, my own need to master the distress led me to ask Kay what it might look like if the confusion was organized. I expected a bland and unrevealing picture, with a simple repetition of the colors in a structured arrangement, in line with Kay's general defensive style of simple repression and denial. Instead, she surprised me out of our mutual despair by painting a woman with war paint, with every element of the first picture converted into something protective. She was beginning to be able to use mastery in fantasy to manage her feelings.

When I asked Kay to tell me about the picture of the warrior woman, she said, "It makes me want to holler and yell . . . go kick some ass." This was the first time she reported feelings, not just content about a picture. For the first time in months I felt some hope that we would find a way for things to be different for her. She then cancelled the next three sessions because she was "just too miserable and depressed, I didn't want to get up," and returned with only two sessions before my own week-long vacation.

When I returned from vacation, Kay painted her fear, showing herself behind bars. "Tell me about the bars," I asked. She responded, "I think Joe threatened to hurt me if I told anyone about what he did." I realized that at eight-years-old, the age when she was molested, she was not physically able to see beyond the bars in the picture, and I remembered that at that time in her life her experience with mother was that feelings were disavowed: "You're not sad, there's nothing to be sad about. . . . Don't be a baby." When I reported my own association to the picture, Kay began crying, but could say only, "Thank you for understanding."

In the next session, as we looked at the little girl behind bars, I noticed she needed help to reach out beyond them. Kay painted a young girl reaching out beyond the bars to someone who was not there and then remembered, that in fifth grade, she spent some weeks crying daily. Her parents made an appointment for her to see a psychologist, but when she woke up the day of the appointment and was not crying they canceled it. She then spent several months being "very bossy and mean with everyone." I commented this seemed to be what Kay tried to do in her adult life, to be strong and not let anyone know about her tears, to not be a baby, but inside was the little girl with the tears and the fear.

If the girl could see outside the bars, she would see a path with a stream and flowers, but could not reach it. We spent some sessions exploring the stream and what might be behind the prettiness. As we did so, however, Kay let me know I was not attending to her by beginning again to feel trapped. I understood this as my having joined in on the "nothing to be sad about" defense of Kay's mother and, later, Kay herself. I asked her to paint herself again, and she painted herself as solid black, in shackles that could only be released by someone else. She was trapped in her dilemma: she no longer wanted to disavow the feelings that were real, but did not want to experience the anger, pain, and fear. The shackles seemed to hold her feelings at bay. We talked about whether there might be a way to contain the feelings while she went on a brief vacation, so she could enjoy herself. She painted a fence around the shackled figure and with me standing by the gate with a key.

My experience within the analysis was, for the most part, that I did not have to struggle to find something to explore with Kay. Almost always, the pictures she painted offered some element I was curious about and could ask her to elaborate on, or to associate to. When I found myself without such a question, or needed to take time overnight to find such a question or comment, I realized, we strayed off the path that was true to her and had wandered onto a path that met my needs rather than hers. At those times—and frequently within the overall analysis—I shared with her my sense of a dead end and we would go back to the last picture she identified as truly reflecting something about herself. She seemed to increasingly recognize which pictures represented her, whereas she previously she took my word without a sense of connection for herself.

When she returned from her vacation, we returned to the image of Kay as trapped. I asked her to paint something that felt "real," and she painted herself tangled inextricably in her fear and depression. This is what kept her from turning her feelings into "war paint," to find some effective defenses. I asked how old she was when she first began to be so tangled up and she said, with no hesitation, three, when her brother was born. She did not like him and wanted her parents to take him back to the hospital. She thinks this may have been the first time she was told not to feel what she felt.

Around this time, as I shared with Kay the experience of feeling stuck again, I realized how little I really knew about the facts of her life and we reviewed the major incidents in her life together. As we explored this, it became clear the defensive "tangling up" began at age three. The molestation by her uncle began at about age eight and continued every few months until she was twelve, when she pushed him away. She felt, at that time, she was "tangled" too much in her unhappiness to move emotionally any more than to defend herself. By sixteen the defensive "tangling," and her emotional paralysis, was almost complete. At twenty, she lived with a boyfriend and was in art school when he was arrested for drug use. She fled home to her parents, dropped out of art school, and took a job doing piece work. In that job her obsessive compulsive perfectionism did not allow her to work fast, so she was made an inspector, making good use of the defensive perfectionism. Subsequently she gave up using her art to express herself, but learned to teach, using it for others and to earn money.

Kay, we both knew, started her emotional tangle and constriction in order to protect herself from something internal and I asked her to paint what it protected her from. She painted her anger, very much like the early images of her self, but without the confining black box. It looked like a shield to me and we explored this image briefly, finding manageable pieces.

Shortly after this, I asked Kay to paint herself before Uncle Joe. She painted a picture of a cheerful, happy young girl of about three- or four-years-old, waving at someone. When I asked what that young girl might make of her anger at being hurt at eight, Kay painted a princess, who turned everything into jewels. I commented that jewels are useless for protection and asked what the warrior woman of the earlier picture might turn the colors of the anger into. Initially, Kay said flowers. With encouragement to imagine something not only pretty but useful, she decided they might be a shield. Then she added that the cheerful, happy young girl was dead; Joe and all the hiding of her feelings had killed her.

Kay and I spent several sessions talking about the ways the young girl she was had inhibited herself as she tried to be safe, remembering the tangles that kept her from doing anything. We recognized that when she returned home at twenty, fleeing from the emotional intensity of life with her boyfriend, she reinforced the inhibitions. Tearfully, Kay said "What Joe did kept me from being what I'm supposed to be. . . ." I asked if she could paint her anger and grief at that loss, if she could use it instead of letting it tangle her up. She cried, saying she did not know but would try, and was unable to.

Kay seemed increasingly more able to see the pictures as metaphors for herself. I searched for ways to help her harness the power in her anger and commented on the difference between the warrior woman and the beautiful, but not strong, princess with jewels. I asked Kay to paint what the warrior woman has that the princess does not. She painted a prepubertal girl in armor with a mace. This picture originally was in black and white, but later she added vibrant color.

I remarked something had changed for Kay between our first eighteen months of mostly verbal treatment and her return after the break in her treatment when the verbal approach was not useful. When I first met her, she felt empty and unhappy, but not disabled. She could only imagine her progressive decline was because of the troubles she had with male-female relationships and the loss of her boyfriend. We talked about her sense that one could be powerful and safe, or pretty and loved but helpless, but that it was not possible to be both powerful and loved.

As Kay was able to imagine protection from the dangers in life—to imagine saying no to them—she began to articulate the damage done by her earlier inability to speak her reality. She was not sure it was possible to say no without destroying the relationship with the other, but was learning to use fantasy and unconscious processes to defend against uncomfortable feelings, as she learned from very early on that language can be used to hide from and to lie to others about uncomfortable events.

I reminded Kay loneliness and feeling unloved is awful—almost as awful for her as what happened with Joe—but knowing the truth allows you to imagine change. We agreed she was learning she could be something other than a victim. When I asked what the young warrior's colors would be, they were the red of anger, the purple of fear, and the orange of life and passion.

I told Kay I thought she did not know how to let the hurting part of herself communicate with the adult functioning part of herself. When she acknowledged the pain, she was unable to function, because she could only protect the adult part of herself by shutting it out. We spent several days exploring visual metaphors of how she might let the parts of herself communicate. She created an image of two people, her and me, with the blue of my peace, accepting, and understanding, and the black of her pain to neutralize it and keep it from taking over. Her final image looked somewhat like a yin/yang image. It was only later I realized she painted herself and me, not (or, perhaps, also?) the two parts of herself, and she was likely still experiencing things within the safety of the therapeutic hold, not yet able to think of herself as on her own unless abandoned.

About eighteen months into the art phase of her treatment, Kay told me clearly that, although the pictures came from her, they did not come close to expressing how she actually felt. Sometimes the picture with the swirling fear and confusion felt real to her, but the hopefulness I saw in the warrior woman was most often completely foreign to Kay. I asked her to paint a picture about herself that was true to herself. It included black, her pain and unhappiness, but not solid black. There was some angry red, again not solid, but in pieces; some green of life trying to get in; some blue of "a more normal life" trying to enclose the anger and pain; and some pinkish purple, the "wild crazy" part of herself trying to have a little excitement. As we looked at the image, she imagined the black would fall off and disappear, but I commented the black seemed necessary in the picture to provide structure: it could be positive if kept under control. I remembered the bars from an earlier picture that both supported and constrained the young girl reaching out.

Kay and I spent some time trying to explore the connections between feelings and words. It was clear she still had trouble connecting the two. We were not able to find our own meanings for the abstract nouns about sadness, happiness, or fear. Her language was beginning to be useful to reflect emotions and to establish connections, but did not yet have a useful life of its own within her. She was able to paint images for each word—safe: a door to shut out danger; happy: a child swinging from a tree; angry: throwing things—but when I asked her to put together "sad" and "family" she could not. I asked her to paint something about herself with feeling and she painted herself melting away, disappearing. When I asked what would stop the melting away, Kay painted green life growing up around it, holding it, and supporting it.

In childhood, as we learn to talk about our internal experience, we learn miscommunications and misunderstandings happen when we do so. This reinforces the awareness of our separateness from others, and the capacity to manage oneself autonomously—without the mother-child "merger" of early infancy—is strained. The fact that I saw hope and support where Kay saw only pain, and that I saw the hopeful image of a strong woman unrelated to Kay's own sense of self. This strained our connection, but also introduced the possibility of other views of her life.

As we continued to look for ways to identify and communicate Kay's internal experience, I asked her to paint the two warrior women—the adult with war paint and the twelve-year-old in armor—doing something together. The painting clearly was of women ready for battle. T (the warrior woman) has anger for a shield, L (for Kay's middle name) has fear for both a shield and a spear; and they are ready to battle against the black that holds them back. I asked her to paint the battle, and she used red (anger), green (life), joy (yellow), and orange (passion). In describing what she painted, she said, "The spear (fear) releases life, joy, and passion when it strikes, and the mace releases anger at the black." After the battle they pick up the debris, then (as I asked about what they would do during my upcoming break) they go skinny dipping. Kay was able to laugh with me about these images and share a sense of relief and relaxation as I left for another vacation.

When I returned, I had an early version of this paper for Kay to read. She reported it seemed mostly true, and her only comment was, "You're right, I never really learned to use words to talk about my feelings." Within the next few weeks she brought in a dream that introduced the next phase of the therapy.

In the dream, Kay walked through the halls of a school, like the one where she taught. There was no one there but her and the floors were covered with a sticky papier-mâché substance made by the children in the school. She wandered aimlessly and there were no particular feelings involved.

I asked Kay to paint the dream and she was at pains to create a particular color of blue for the "sticky stuff." She mixed two blues, the blue she used for peace and the blue she used for confusion, to get the right color. She did not realize, until after she finished, what the colors meant. Kay found a stage with a door, but could not get out because it was locked so she and returned to the halls. Together we introduced the warrior women to the halls. As they walked, the "sticky stuff" disappeared, and eventually they found a door, chained and locked. The warrior women broke open the door and entered a room filled with gray people, who were frightened of the warrior women and their color.

At this point in the treatment, Kay was again exhausted and felt, at times, unable to get out of bed, even to come to therapy. She felt even more stuck and hopeless. I commented, as I did at other times of brief stalemate, on my belief that the stuckness might mean we were going down a path that was not true for her, but one chosen by me. I tried to pull back and be less directive.

Until now, Kay's images were two dimensional, although, at times, it seemed to me a three dimensional expression might provide more information. I found some Play Doh in multiple colors and brought it in. Kay, for the first time, used Play Doh to create this scene. She made the back wall of the room, which had no exit except the door by which the warrior women entered, and there were multiple little gray people in the room.

We again continued to explore the image and the response of the little gray people to the colorful warrior women. As the little gray people touched the warrior women, some of them took on color. Some took the color on permanently, some only temporarily. Yet others remained gray. I found myself wanting to help the gray people to take on color and to leave the room, as Kay made it quite clear that many of them were afraid to do so. As I considered, I mused out loud about what might help the gray people leave the room, and I suddenly realized that was *my* need, not Kay's. I told her I was being pushy again and I needed to be quiet and let them (the gray people and, of course, Kay) decide for themselves what to do. She laughed, agreeing, and I was silent for the remainder of the session. My recognition of my counter-transference need to see "progress" also allowed me to be silent most of the time after that.

With the Play Doh and no prompts from me, Kay first made a lily pad and koi fish, then a Buddha, an image of herself sleeping, and an *on-sen*, a Japanese meditation pool where males and females soak in different sides of the pool. Each image carried a sense of peace and calm. With the peaceful but emotionally lifeless images, she also made a lily bud growing out of the "mucky dirt," but with potential for beauty, and told me it represented herself, rooted in dirt and awfulness but with potential.

Some days later, after another silent period, Kay made an image of a beach, with land, people inland, and a boat on the beach. Next she made a lagoon with coconut trees, bushes, sand, water, and a boat in the lagoon, but no people. Again, there was a sense of peace and calm: there was a volcano on a distant island, but with the lava flow away from the lagoon and, thus, safe. Each time she did not comment except to describe the image.

I continued to sit quietly after a description of each image and, next, Kay made a boat on choppy water. She then, in the same session, made a coral reef and a shipwreck. She said waves dragged the boat over the coral reef, which broke it up, and the person in the boat was shipwrecked and lying unconscious on the shore.

As we contemplated this image, it was quite clear to both of us that Kay was the victim of the shipwreck. I experienced a profound feeling of despair and helplessness. Initially, I gave voice to that feeling, but then was able to maintain silence as the despair continued for several weeks. During this time, Kay was severely depressed, at times unable even to get out of bed for her session and to do little else. She began a course of acupuncture, which was recommended to her by a friend.

Eventually Kay moved again in our sessions and made a raft from the shipwreck, using the shipwreck victim's shirt as a sail, and was able to venture out into the water. Shortly thereafter, the shipwreck victim was picked up by two women in another boat and rescued. Kay was quite clear the two women were the acupuncturist and me. We both knew the woman in the images was Kay, although we talked about her sometimes as Kay and sometimes as a third party, depending on how connected Kay felt to the images.

The women landed on an island where the acupuncturist treated Kay while I rested. In the next image, the acupuncturist and I conferred about what to do while Kay rested. Kay then went exploring on the island, found another boat, and went out on her own, leaving us on the island. She took a Buddha and the spear she had from the early warrior woman, but left the two helpers and a boat so we were not stranded.

As she explored alone, Kay made several side trips: one to a small atoll where she found a lotus bud and some coral, and one to another small island where she found her paramour on a flying carpet. Eventually she came to an island with many orchids (an image which occurred to her in one of her reveries without associations). Attracted by the orchids, she landed and began to explore, finding in the undergrowth a Buddhist temple with Chinese characters on the roof that meant "something profound." Initially, Kay did not know what the characters meant, but a few minutes later she said "Happiness keeps coming to mind. . . . The Inn of Orchid Happiness."

Kay believed she was on the island to learn, but she did not know what she was to learn. Her associations included orchids losing their blooms in the fall, which is sad, but on the island they always bloomed. The stupa, or temple, was what drew her to the island, and the orchids drew her to leave the boat. The monk drew her to the temple and her association was to a phrase "inward and onward," from *The Chronicles of Narnia* (Lewis, 1950), where it means increasing self-knowledge and enlightenment.

The temple was not enclosed, but allowed movement, in and out, from the inside to the world. She speculated that might be what the monk was to teach her, to be able to move from within herself to engage in the wider world.

At this point, we entered into another period of "stuckness," with little movement and an increase in Kay's depression. After about six weeks, she seemed to feel better and returned to contemplation of the stupa, the Inn of Orchid Happiness. We speculated that the orchids might represent her art, as a road to her happiness. Late in that session she said an image came to her, but she did not know what it meant. The image was of a melting figure with blood pouring out of various spots in the body, perhaps out of the chakras used in her acupuncture. The title of the figure was "No More to Go."

The figure, as she drew it, stood with its head back. She modeled it out of Play Doh later and it sat in a lotus position in a pool of blood. My own association was of a voluntary pouring out of one's heart's blood and Kay immediately agreed with that thought. This image was not associated with any emotional pain I could identify and she agreed.

Over the next four to six months, Kay seemed unable to continue the work. She could not generate any more images, and attempts to talk about the stupa or the meaning of it led nowhere. Kay asked for a reduction in the frequency of sessions, as she did not want to withdraw from the therapy but found it exhausting and unproductive. I was unclear about the meaning of this development, but felt it was important to acknowledge her wishes and her will, as her mother had not done, and I agreed to the plan. We met every two weeks and, in those sessions, worked much as we had done previously. I did not sense a significant difference in the tone of the sessions, or in the productiveness of the work.

After a few months of this shift in the process, Kay and I talked about our mutual sense that we might have come to a natural changing point in our relationship. I remembered when we were stuck in this way previously; the shift from two dimensional to three dimensional art was helpful. I asked what other art techniques might be useful. After discussing several possibilities, we agreed collages seemed a possible route and we agreed to try a technique where Kay would make a collage and I would respond to it. I brought some supplies from a local art store—stiff paper for the collages, possible things to include, magazines—and Kay provided scissors and a glue stick.

Kay's process, simple but potentially profound, was to look through a magazine, tear or cut out images or phrases that struck her, and then glue them on a piece of stiff paper. As she described it, she might not know what would emerge until all the pieces were included on the final project. I then asked her to tell me about it. Initially, she could only describe what was on the paper without associations, much as she did at first with her paintings. Later she was able to add thoughts and comments.

I tried as best I could to follow the same procedure, responding to what she showed in the collage, as well as what she said about it. This mode of communicating did seem to reawaken our ability to communicate more than feeling stuck. Kay's images, initially, were primarily about her depression, her despair, her sense of fatigue, and being overwhelmed, while my images were primarily about hope, opening doors, and allowing oneself to play. At one point, Kay did a collage that was almost entirely about the "shoulds" and "oughts" in her life and how burdened she felt. It was increasingly clear she was shackled by her need to be "good" and she had little sense of ability to play or even that it was acceptable to play.

I saw this process as an unusual way of free-associating together and sharing our associations with each other. Kay's inability to use language to convey her internal experience was initially profound, but lessened slowly as we used art together to communicate, first in two and then in three dimensions. The collages, most of which were accompanied by words, seemed to be a transitional space that encompassed both her art and my verbal orientation. It allowed us to speak in a language we shared, a sort of "Creole" (a fully developed language that originates as a pidgin). I believe it represents a developmental step toward a fuller, emotionally useful ability to use language to communicate one's internal experience to others, along with the internal shifts in psychic structure that accompany that growing ability.

At this writing, Kay's treatment continues. We are aware that art is available, but for now we seem to be able to connect and communicate through words in a way that does allow her some access to her inner experience.

Kay's treatment showed me how much we take for granted about the language that is the medium of our work. We assume adults who come into treatment are able to tell us about their inner selves. We expect defensive distortions, repression, denial, and resistance to knowing the self, but we do not expect the words used will be empty of information about our patient's unconscious processes. Recognizing Kay's words did not initially reflect her inner self led me to want to know more about how language becomes the medium as well as the message.

Chapter Two

Bringing Meaning to Words in Psychotherapy

Kay taught me we cannot take for granted that people with apparently intact language have the ability to use it to describe themselves. They may be unable to observe their internal world, to "mentalize" (Fonagy, Gergely, Jurist, and Target, 2005). Individuals without a self-reflective capacity often have trouble managing their behaviors in general—in emotion regulation, in interacting appropriately with others—and so I thought about the many children I see in my child psychiatric and psychoanalytic practice that struggle to learn to "use their words" instead of hitting or yelling or doing other things our society frowns upon. Reflecting on my experiences with children's learning to "use their words" quickly led me to remember Susan.

When I met Susan, I was in my last year of child psychiatric training in a program that emphasized the importance of the acquisition of insight through verbal interchange in the therapeutic process: the essence of the "talking cure." She was then nine-years-old and had been in treatment for five years prior to our first meeting. Her presenting problems at age five included biting peers in nursery school, clinging to her mother, social withdrawal, immature language development, and confused verbalization of her thoughts. Her early history was full of descriptions of delays in motor and language development, intense clinginess to mother, and refusal to play with peers. Between ages two and five, some improvements were noted after Susan developed a close relationship with grandfather. He died when she was four, however, and at that point she again became intensely clingy and bizarre. When she was brought to treatment at age five, her language was perseverative and echolalic, with loose associations and what the notes from the time describe as a predominance of primary process thought. She was very anxious with intense fears of oral rage and retaliation (this language is also taken from contemporaneous records). The diagnostic terminology used at the initial evaluation was childhood psychosis with symbiotic features. Today we would likely say she suffered from psychosis not otherwise specified, or from a moderately severe pervasive developmental disorder.

At the time I worked with her, Susan had been in a special education classroom and in twice-weekly psychotherapy, as part of a partial hospitalization program, for four years. In addition, her parents engaged in weekly child-centered therapy, focused on helping them to find ways to manage her behavior, understand her as much as possible, and help them deal with the stress Susan's behaviors caused the family. Medication was not useful. During the first four years of her treatment, there was significant improvement and Susan was finally discharged from the partial hospital program at the beginning of my work with her. The parents continued in child-centered therapy, while Susan attended psychotherapy sessions twice weekly with me after her previous therapist left the area.

Academically, Susan functioned at or slightly below grade level in all areas, with an IQ of 89 (up from 59 at age 5). Socially, she functioned only moderately well with frequent inappropriate behaviors such as impulsively kissing comparative strangers and occasional brief psychotic regressions. At the beginning of the year that Susan and I worked together her communications within the treatment hour were very primitive and chaotic, although she was able to limit her behavior and was not generally a behavior management problem.

Understanding my work with Susan requires that we consider not only how Susan was functioning, but my own attitude and abilities at the time. I was just beginning the last year of my training and considered myself competent in psychotherapy with adults and adolescents. I had some experience with children, most of whom were less disturbed than Susan, and felt I understood how to approach establishing a relationship with her. I started with new supervisors at the beginning of the year and was, of course, eager to demonstrate I was capable and could do the work. At the same time, I was quite aware I still had a great deal to learn, that I could not expect things to go smoothly; but I believed with the help of my supervisor I would be able to be helpful to this very disturbed young girl. I kept "process notes"—detailed notes that came as close as possible to verbatim reports of our interactions, completed immediately after the session—so that I could talk with my supervisor about the work. The session reported here is the sixth of twice weekly forty-five minute sessions, far enough into the year that Susan and I recognized each other and knew a little about each other.

As I greeted Susan in the waiting room, she came with me cheerfully, saying "You're beautiful, I like you." Throughout the session she repeatedly told me she liked me, usually without any perceptible connection to what had gone on before. She seated herself at my desk, as was her habit, and doodled, drawing squares and making scribbles that seemed to be without either content or meaning, even for Susan. As she talked, she made disconnected statements about broken legs and the use of crutches, was ink poisonous? was water poisonous? was she strong? was she stronger than S (her sister)? and so on. I attempted to respond by connecting her comments to the context of our relationship, including the recent change of therapist, labeling her remarks as expressing anxiety about safety and about being "broken." I also, at times, simply commented on what she was doing, describing her actions and maintaining a running commentary (Etezady, 2011) in an attempt to find a communicative flow when I did not know what she was thinking or feeling. For example, "You're drawing, making lots of squares."

After about twenty minutes of this, Susan noticed some "snowmen" made from brown clay on my desk and asked for the clay. I stood to reach and hand her the clay, but she did nothing with it. As I sat down again, she continued to scribble, then took all the paper clips out of the holder on my desk and scattered them over the desk. As she played with the paper clips aimlessly and scribbled some more, she began talking about a baby who "poopies in her pants. Is poopie hot? Is fart hot? Do you doodoo in your pants?" I listened, still trying to find a communicative thread, responding to most remarks in some noncommittal way. Throughout, Susan smiled and laughed nervously and occasionally asked me a question, which I was able to answer such as "Do you make mistakes?" (after I acknowledged my misunderstanding of one of her remarks). There were further questions about poisons, about Susan's strength (with insistence that I feel her biceps), about my own strength. I struggled to find meaning in this material so I could respond with verbal clarifications (Etezady, 2011), as I believed was the proper technique. For example, "No, ink isn't good to swallow, but it's not poisonous. You're really worrying a lot about what things can hurt you."

As this disorganized interaction continued, Susan became even less organized and began talking about playing with feces, asking "Do your lips get stinky when you say 'poopie'?" When our time was up, I said we needed to stop. She was able to reorganize and behave reasonably appropriately on the way back to and in the waiting room and held my hand as we went. My office, however, was left looking as if someone had made a concerted effort to scatter as many small things as possible over the surface of the desk.

The chaotic, disconnected flavor of this session was typical, to the point I found myself almost unable to write process notes for many sessions, because I could identify no current themes or connections between behavioral associations, which might help me organize and remember the session. As a beginning child therapist, I responded to Susan's behavior with anxiety and intense efforts to find some coherence in the material, building on formulations found in the chart, from previous therapists. Most of my thoughts and tentative understandings started with our relationship, but I was not generally able to progress beyond a somewhat generic formulation that Susan was anxious about our relationship and about safety.

The progress of Susan's therapy over this year is difficult to follow if one attends only to the details of the verbal communications. Each session appeared to have little connection to the last and each seemed disorganized, with little connection between Susan's remarks. The overall theme, I thought, was chaos, which I believed at the time was by its very nature uninterpretable. I did continue to try to find some thread of meaning to put into words and my supervisor helped me think about the material as we searched together for that thread of meaning. My supervisor also helped me tolerate the anxiety I felt at not knowing and not understanding.

I realized in later years, reviewing my notes from Susan's treatment, that when we attend to the *mode* of communication in the hours, the process becomes clearer. At the beginning of the year, Susan seldom or never made direct statements about her thoughts or feelings. The verbal remarks she made were usually somewhat bizarre and could not be understood directly. Instead, Susan's communication was through her behavior, as in the session described above. My therapeutic interventions focused on finding meaning and translating those behavioral communications into statements about Susan's internal state. For example, "You keep asking if I am poisonous; maybe you're afraid I'm going to hurt you." I structured my interventions around my sketchy understanding of Susan, but it was often difficult for me to know from her productions if I was correct or not. I did take personal comfort from an ability to find organization through the formulations.

As the months went on, Susan was able to talk in small increments about her thoughts and feelings, naming herself as angry, or sad, or happy. These remarks were always brief and she seldom followed up with any discussion of the feelings. Normal life stresses, especially around separation, threatened Susan's new ability to label her internal reality, but it could be recouped with assistance. One example of the process of regression and loss of this new ability, and then recovery within a session, happened at the first session after Thanksgiving break (about five months after we first met).

Susan's habit was to hold my hand as we walked to my office. On this day, however, she greeted me in the waiting room with a panicky flight from me, saying, "You're poisonous! Don't touch me! Don't touch me!" She was willing to come to the office only if I did not touch her. She made some disconnected comments about the family's Thanksgiving and about not having seen me the previous week. Because I was thinking about separation issues, I decided she might be mad at me for not accompanying her on the family's Thanksgiving vacation. I verbalized for Susan that because she was so mad at me, she thought I must be angry at her too. And if I was angry at her, she was afraid I was poisonous and wanted to hurt her. When I said this to Susan, she calmed her panic, stopped avoiding me, and slowly returned to our more usual patterns of interaction. At the end of the hour she hugged me, saying "I love you," as she often did. Both my own anxiety—what do you do if you cannot even get your patient into the office?—and Susan's panic were contained and transformed by the use of words to communicate what I thought she was feeling and wanted me to know.

Over the months, Susan began spontaneously to mention she was angry, or sad, or happy, without fragmentation. She followed that by identifying what the origin of the feeling was. Her ability to establish and experience some connectedness within the session, both interpersonally and intrapsychically, also changed over the year. Early in the year, her verbal communications were severely disorganized: rambling, seemingly unconnected comments about poison, relative strengths, crutches, etc. Communication and connectedness seemed to be primarily through touch and affect. In the third month she began to verbally attribute emotion—anger and sadness—to Kermit the Frog or other toys in the office and to tell stories with them. In about the sixth month (after the Thanksgiving break) she occasionally acknowledged that she felt something other than happy. Slowly, as she began to talk more and to be less disorganized, her behaviors in all areas improved. The impulsive behaviors that were problematic at school and home were decreasing and she was more able to accept adult direction and limits. I understood this as gradually increasing intrapsychic structure. In the last month of our work together, as we anticipated my leaving and the coming of yet another therapist, Susan was able to say, very directly, that she was afraid her mother preferred her sister and that she would miss me and was sad I was leaving.

At the beginning of my year of work with Susan, she used indirect, behavioral communication that required me to guess at and assume meanings for her communications almost all the time. At some time in the fourth or fifth month she began to make more direct statements, which allowed me to have some certainty about what she felt. Initially, the comments had to do with the feelings of the toys she played with, as she told stories about them, but fairly quickly she began to make "I-statements," about her own feelings. After only a few sessions with direct statements about herself, she began using American Sign Language or writing, but no verbal speech, for these "I-statements." Susan taught herself ASL from an encyclopedia article on the deaf, and for two months, in each session she would tell me in sign or in writing, "I love you." Although she spoke the same words earlier and did so again in later sessions, she could not at this point. In retrospect, some years ago, I decided she was trying to provide emotional distance, through an additional layer of cognitive unraveling to the communication. Now I also wonder if perhaps she was testing to see if it was really true that behavior has meaning and if I was really willing to work to find out what she meant.

As I worked with Susan on finding words for her feelings, we began to be able to talk about how strong feelings were disorganizing for her, saying when she felt something very strongly she "thought funny." At the end of my year with her, as I left the training program and prepared Susan for yet another change in therapist, she expressed her anxiety about her new therapist: "Will she be able to help me talk about thinking funny?" She was able to say she would miss me, she wanted to write me, and she worried about who the new therapist would be.

In the first years after I finished my training and left Susan, it was clear she found it valuable to have a way to label and view her internal chaos, and that the labels I provided helped to contain them. As one of my early supervisors said, the best way to reduce the intensity of an emotion within a therapy session (or at any time) is to put it into words. Susan learned this lesson well and she was concerned her new skill, which allowed her to contain the chaos, would be lost as she lost the therapist with whom she shared that skill.

Susan made enormous progress during her first four years of treatment. In the fifth year of treatment, the year with me, her progress was visible almost month to month. In my attempt to understand what allowed this striking change, I began with my original assumption, that the content of the interpretations, especially around object loss, were the key. Most of my comments to Susan throughout the year were about feelings I expected she would experience when people were absent, or when they were angry, or when her interactions with them were troublesome to her. As I reviewed the material years later, in light of further experience, I noticed Susan's problems lay primarily in the area of maintaining ego boundaries, and of remembering who she was when under affective stress (e.g., saying "I love you" or when angry). Her progress was in containing and modulating her affect with verbal expression of feelings, developing into a basic tension-regulating technique. Both content and form of my interventions seemed crucial in fostering this development in Susan: the use of words, accompanied by my own ability to tolerate the affect without disorganization, provided for Susan a type of intrapsychic tool to use in structuring and tolerating the affect aroused by the events in her life.

Tolpin (1971) describes the developmental process that parallels this clinical process. She suggests in normal development, when the infant has as yet no capacity to manage anxiety, mother's buffering function operates to reduce the panic-like reaction to sensory over-stimulation. Language plays a role in the buffering function, as mother labels a particular state of tension ("Oh, you look sad today") and remains calm.

As language grows and development progresses the infant's ability to use self-soothing grows. Gradually, the child begins to substitute his own skill for mother's soothing, buffering activities. In the same way that mother "lends" her ability to soothe the infant when needed, the mother or the therapist may "lend" her ability to find meaning to the child or the patient when needed. Lack of an adequate relationship with mother will prevent internalization of this function and will interfere with the development of psychic structure.

The infant's progress from indistinct babbling to "mama," with the ability to recognize mother as separate from others, generally parallels the development of the mother-infant bond. The mother's pleasure in the babbling and words will then stimulate further language and cognitive development and strengthen the relationship. As the mother-infant bond develops along with speech, the use of words to organize one's experience allows for a sense of self and environmental mastery. "Words when spoken have a concretizing effect as they provide labels, shape, and control over affects and previously ill-defined fantasies. . . . The more the child's cognitive development, as reflected in the child's language, proceeds, the easier it will be for the child to understand his or her feelings and make connections" (Lewis, 1977, p. 658–59).

The connections the child makes are between external events and intrapsychic phenomena, such as feelings or fantasies. The fantasies and affects are labeled, shaped, and controlled through a gradual process that parallels the process by which an abstract symbol, such as a word, becomes attached to an experiential state. As a particular state of tension is experienced repetitively and accompanied by labels (e.g., "Oh, you look sad today."), the labeling does two things. (1) It allows meaning to develop by repetitive association of the infant's experiential state with the label and (2) it allows a mental representation of that state, a memory of sorts, less overwhelming than the state itself, to form. That mental representation, a nonverbal experiential gestalt, can be called up by a signal word or phrase. The experiential gestalt called up by the signal word includes the experience of mother's soothing presence, so the "memory" of the feeling is not overwhelming. This allows for the conversion of global anxiety into a more focused signal-like anxiety.

With further growth the ego develops its own ability to soothe; the signal-like anxiety associated with mother's presence becomes true signal anxiety and mother (and her ability to soothe with words) becomes internalized. Once mother's presence is internalized, the child will be able to "self-soothe," to calm herself without mother's intervention. Lack of an adequate relationship with mother or a similar caretaker will prevent internalization of the soothing function and interfere with the development of psychic structure.

Early in my professional practice, after completing my training, I would have said the first four years of Susan's therapy seem to represent a "corrective symbiotic experience" (Mahler, 1975, p. 167), that the positive and accepting merger states with her sequential therapists allowed Susan to begin to develop ego boundaries and maintain them through affective storms, as well as to contain and regulate weaker affects. She used transitional objects (such as sunglasses which "remind me of my grandfather"), developed consistent use of pronouns, and later was able to relinquish the transitional objects as she developed an ability to regulate affect enough to remember her therapist through separation and her resulting anger. Thus, she moved "toward object constancy" (Mahler, 1975, p. 120). Gradually she reached a stage where she was able to retain a more or less cohesive mental representation of herself—a sense of self—even under the stress of anger and threatened psychotic regression.

In the fifth year of Susan's therapy, I would have said, my use of words and cognitive explanations of behavior served a buffering function, allowing me to modulate my own tension about whether I could help Susan. This buffering within the therapeutic "symbiosis," by analogy with Mahler's 1975 description of the maternal symbiosis, was extended to Susan. In the therapeutic dyad, I functioned as an auxiliary ego or perhaps a self-object, allowing Susan's panic to be transformed instead into signal anxiety. Later in therapy, when Susan used sign language and writing to communicate, as well as using specific organizing phrases ("thinking funny" to refer to panicky ego fragmentation), the words seemed to serve as a "transitional form of mental structure that then is destined to become a part of the child's own structure which maintain [sic] his cohesiveness" (Tolpin, 1971, p. 319).

Thus Susan learned to verbalize her emotions (affects) as a way to control them. Not only did words help her to shape and control affects and fantasies, but ". . . when words and experiences are linked . . . a reorganization of experiences also occurs. Spoken language in interpretation, however briefly it is used, also appears to have a special effect—it serves as an instrument for a rapprochement with elemental feelings and may, thereby, be the means by which a reorganization of inner feelings occurs" (Lewis, 1977, p. 658). Susan gradually learned that words can serve two functions. (1) They can maintain a connection with the (self-) object whose presence is necessary for internal cohesiveness and (2) they can, in themselves, help both to express and to modulate (contain by giving structure to) affect, which is overwhelming when unstructured.

The crucial point of this year appears to have been around Thanksgiving, with the recognition of Susan's rage at being separated from me, the recognition that she and I both survived, and the experience that the feelings could be labeled and thus contained. This experience came at a time when Susan was beginning to be able to recognize and verbalize emotions in general, but not yet attribute them to herself. After the pivotal session, repeated references to it were used to illustrate Susan's difficulties, providing a way of verbalizing and understanding what happened inside her as well as outside: "When you feel something really strongly, sometimes you start to think funny." The repeated memory of this specific experience, taken with other similar memories, allowed the gradual accretion of meaning to originally non-meaningful words such as "angry" and "anxious," so she now had a way to talk about and organize internal events. As she organized the internal events, they became less stressful and she could tolerate strong affects with little or no psychotic regression.

Today, as I consider Susan's therapy, I would not disagree with the above discussion. I would, however, add another crucial element, my confidence that somewhere order existed. Susan's words could be understood for content, but they did not make relational sense—they were not the sorts of questions or comments we generally expect from a child trying to tell us something. Perhaps the experience of being in a relationship with someone who believed her words could be understood beyond the surface content, and who persistently searched for that understanding, allowed Susan to develop the awareness that relationships can be comprehended, and that words can make sense of the relationship over and above the superficial content. Perhaps Susan was able to create for herself, to internalize, several things: First, a sense that the self exists in relationship to others; second, the words we speak affect and reflect that relationship; and third, it is possible to search for and occasionally find that meaning. If this is true, the *content* of my remarks, for one so severely impaired, was almost irrelevant. It did not matter to Susan whether I told her she was angry, or she worried about being safe, or she was sad. What mattered to Susan, as to all of us, was that the world makes sense and that we have a way to find that sense for ourselves. It seems apparent that for Susan, and I believe for many of us, language offers a way to find that sense.

Chapter Three

Form Follows Function

Language allows us to understand the world around us. It connects us with others, but we also use it to hide from them, to keep secrets, and to lie. Language makes it possible to live in the world of Others and to find the space we need in our relationships. It allows us to choose which parts of our internal world we wish to share with others and which parts we wish to conceal. As psychoanalysts and psychotherapists know, however, the context in which language occurs may also reveal parts of our internal world: In the words of Eduardo Krapf (1955), "the form of linguistic expression is just as worthy of psychoanalytic research as its content" (p. 343). Thomas Ogden (1997) has also explored some of the "effects created *in language* . . . a dimension of language usage in which the creation and communication of meanings/feelings is indirect, that is, relatively independent of what is being said (at the level of the semantic content of language)" (p. 15). In this chapter, I describe some (but certainly not all) of the ways the *form* of our language, as much as the *content*, communicates meaning and shapes our relatedness with others.

LILY, AARON, AND BARBARA

Lily

For Lily, most of her early communication with me was through its form. She used her language mostly to conceal and there was a great deal of it. Early in her treatment I wondered whether she suffered from logorrhea or hypergraphia, since she talked and wrote rapidly and nonstop, but without saying much that was useful. She brought in sheets and sheets of written material that was disjointed, tangential, and difficult to follow. If I wrote down the words in the hour, it would also have been sheets and sheets of disjointed, tangential, and difficult to follow material. It seemed clear she was anxious, but I could not get a handle on what made her anxious, and she spoke so rapidly and intensely it was very difficult for me to interrupt even to clarify that she was anxious. She anxiously made appointments and then anxiously canceled because of unanticipated conflicts. Once, she rescheduled three times in two days.

I found myself withdrawing from Lily, both within my head and in our interaction. I set limits on talking with her outside of appointments, set limits on providing prescriptions for medications to manage her anxiety, set limits in many different ways. During her hours, I found myself drifting, thinking about almost anything except Lily. It often felt as if I was being washed away by waves of chaotic, meaningless noise.

When I tried to think about Lily in a way that allowed me actually to process—in words, using my analytic self to sort out her primary process behavior—I was unable to. I could not find a way to describe how she behaved, or how I felt. I believed if I could describe it to someone, I could find a way to think about how to be helpful, but I kept getting washed away by the chaos.

I tried to think about Lily's chaos as internal structure, as her defense, in an attempt to engage my analytic self to process the relationship and interaction (and of course to withdraw in a useful way). I could not, however, manage to hang onto the concept long enough to frame any questions. I could not manage to engage myself with thinking about Lily except with dread at my incompetence, resignation at the need to listen without hearing anything meaningful, sadness at her suffering and at my inability to relieve it.

Only as I wrote a description of my *own* experience with Lily, was I aware of the re-enactment I was drawn into. I experienced the incompetence, resignation, sadness, and lack of ability to function that Lily herself experienced, which she had experienced through her childhood but was not allowed to articulate. Because she was not allowed to articulate it, she became unable to. As she disallowed my own struggles to articulate her experience, I became unable to articulate it even to myself. I could not find her meaning and I drowned in her words.

Aaron

Aaron required me to struggle to understand in a different way. He talked rapidly, with abrupt shifts of idiom, sentence, and topic. I understood the words he said, but usually felt something was missing that allowed me to make sense of his emotional struggles. As is often the case, I expected if I listened for another few sentences, he would provide the missing piece. So I listened, but the missing pieces never appeared. I was left feeling as if I had missed every third word in his monologues, and that I could not manage to connect fully and helpfully to him. He seemed to find the therapy valuable, but spent most of the time simply talking about what happened in his life, without exploring what the events might mean for him or to him. When I intervened to ask if he had ideas about why he might have done something, or what he felt, or what he thought about a particular event, he was unable to respond in any way that helped me to "fill in the gaps" in his descriptions of his life. He moved from day-to-day of his life with little sense of connection or organization, much as he moved from sentence-to-sentence with little sense of connection or organization.

Barbara

Barbara is a Chinese professional, whom I treated via Skype, an Internet-based video call program that allows face-to-face, real-time interaction from distant locations. Her English is quite good and some years ago she spent several months in America for professional training. She is prominent in her field and is quite bright. She worries about her English, but has been able to read difficult professional articles originally published in English and, in general, does well. As we talked, she occasionally stopped to look up words so as to communicate clearly, and she and I were very clear that we needed to pay attention to the language and cultural issues in our work together. At times we had to find different ways to say what we meant in order to under-stand each other clearly. As I listened to and tried to understand Barbara, it often seemed, initially, that I had not quite reached her emotionally, that we were separated by more than the miles between us.

For each of these patients, the form of their linguistic expression shaped what they communicated, and what I was able to understand, about their internal world. This, in turn, shaped my sense of relatedness to them, below the level of my conscious awareness. In no case was the shaping of the communication conscious. Rather, it was itself shaped by, and was a reflec-tion of, their internal world. For each of them, I needed to think consciously about that communication, about the understanding I derived from it, and about what it meant for the relationship between us in order to be able to be helpful to them.

For Lily, the way that she expressed herself forced me to experience, first-hand, the chaos she lived, providing intense and very immediate infor-mation about her own experience, which she could not articulate herself. For Aaron, who seemed not to have a coherent understanding of himself and of the motivations for his behaviors, his form of communication reflected the fragmentation of his internal sense of self, which could also be seen in the fragmented, dysfunctional life that brought him to treatment. For Barbara, the emotional distance I experienced was closely related to her difficulty in finding "experience-near" words for her emotional life. We eventually realized this difficulty, reflected in the form of her linguistic expression, was shaped not only by Barbara's internal experience, but also by the use of a language that was not native to her.

The obstacles to understanding, which I experienced with Barbara because of the language barrier, are not different in quality than those I saw with Aaron, Lily, and other patients, although they are different in intensity. Examining the ways that the lack of a common "mother tongue" affects interpersonal communication will allow us to look more clearly at the other subtle ways that the *form* of communication can enhance or interfere with our verbal interactions.

PSYCHOTHERAPY WITH OTHER THAN THE MOTHER TONGUE

For Barbara, because English is not her first language, her ability to communicate with me about her experience is constrained and inhibited. That, in turn, inhibited and constrained my interpersonal reaction to her. As every psychotherapist knows, our reactions to our patients arise in reaction to what the patient says to us, but also to how the patient says it. With Lily, Aaron, and Barbara I was aware of feeling inhibited in different ways in the free flow of interaction and communication and, as I became aware of that inhibition, I became more and more aware of how the form of their communication expressed an element of their being.

With Barbara, I retrained my professional "reflexes" about how I used our interaction to understand her, because my previous professional experience with such inhibitions and constraints was with people whose internal world was constricted in some way—either by developmental stage or by particular sorts of pathology. Barbara was also somewhat inhibited in expressing her emotions openly, and it was often difficult to understand what related to the language barrier and what was Barbara's own barrier to communication. She and I both developed a sense of how the language issue affected our relationship and, later in the therapy, she told me her problems with talking about her emotions were not only related to the language difficulty. She was aware others were able to express understanding and empathy with vivid and meaningful words, but she was not able to; she could express her empathy with only gestures and behaviors or with very simple words. She was quite clear, in our work together, that her difficulty with expressing her feelings verbally was not only due to the language barrier, but it was true as a child "when my mother and father did not allow me to show feelings." Her nanny, who did most of the caretaking, was uneducated and "did not have the words for feelings" to allow Barbara to learn those words in an emotionally resonant

way. Barbara and I worked together to understand what parts of our communication were difficult because of the language issues and what parts were
difficult because of her lack of emotionally meaningful words for feelings
even in her own language.

Frequently Barbara and I talked about what is common in terms of Chinese life, how Chinese patterns of behavior may differ from American patterns of behavior, and how Chinese attitudes toward relationships are different from American patterns of relationships. I found, in fact, that there are
not many major differences ascribed only to culture. As Harry Stack Sullivan
said, "We are all much more simply human than otherwise" (1947, p. 7), and
that is certainly true between cultures. Issues of the role of women, how
married adults relate to the parents on each side, how work and social life
interact, certainly fall into the range of what I see in American adults. Eventually, I concluded cultural issues did not contribute materially to the sense of
distance in the relationship with Barbara.

There were some differences for me in how I experienced Barbara's
therapy, as compared to my face-to-face American patients. I found the language I used with her was different in subtle ways, which affected how I
thought about her. Because I am a child and adolescent psychoanalyst, I am
quite used to tailoring my vocabulary to the developmental level of the
individual, and I am aware I also tend to tailor the complexity of the interpretations I make in the same way. As I engage in play with children in play
therapy, I simultaneously "translate," in the back of my mind, into a way of
thinking that allows me to analyze behavior and language and then "retrans-
late" the results of the analysis into whatever the play action is facilitating. I
do not find I have to think consciously about developmental level, because it
is implicit in the play communication. With Barbara, and with a few Chinese
therapists I have supervised using Skype, I find myself thinking about what
their developmental level might be, both professionally and personally. I am
often unsure of how much they understand, because the language may not
reflect clearly what they do know and understand. I "translate" to where I
think they may be, but am never certain and because of the Chinese attitude
toward authority (it's rude to ask questions!) I am often not sure how well
they grasped what I say. I do find myself, at odd moments with Barbara,
aware of the need to simplify my phrasing. For instance, in one exchange I
wanted to say something was "simply" true, but began thinking about the
different meanings of "simple" that might confuse her. I finally ended by
saying the issue was "only" true. If I am not careful with myself, I sometimes
think that because her language is less complex, her thoughts are less complex, even though, on examination, that is quite clearly not true.

The vocabulary we use also becomes something that is consciously, as
well as unconsciously considered. In treating Barbara, I realized that with my
American patients I will often use more primitive, experience-near words for

emotions, in an effort to heighten the affect so it can be discussed with more impact. For instance, I will often say something is "scary," rather than "frightening," because "scary" is a childhood word and carries with it the emotional resonances of the frightened child. For Barbara, however, because she learned "scary" and "frightening" at approximately the same developmental age (as an adult), neither has the emotional resonances I intuitively anticipate for a native English-speaker; both are somewhat intellectualized and distant from her emotional experience. This led to my relationship with Barbara being somewhat more distant and intellectualized than I am used to, particularly in a therapeutic association, where one person is seeking assistance for distress and the other is presumed to have some relief to offer for that distress. It took longer than usual for me to feel the therapeutic alliance with Barbara—the emotional connection—was solid and reliable. Initiall,y I believed the difference might be related to the Chinese attitude toward teachers and social superiors, which is one of extreme respect: it is considered rude to ask questions, one does not challenge the teacher, and one certainly never disagrees with the teacher. Although this was quite evident in Barbara's treatment, I also saw similar attitudes in American patients who needed me to be strong, perfect, and always right. I eventually decided that with Barbara the emotional elements of our relationship were more distant than could be accounted for even by her culture-driven need to be respectful of my authority. I concluded it was related, at least in part, to the fact that Barbara was constrained to use words that, for her, contained only an entirely intellectual meaning, a translation from the more meaningful Chinese into the English that had little or no emotional resonance.

As I think about how the relationship with Barbara progressed and the nature of our therapeutic alliance, it seems our initial difficulty in solidly establishing the relationship was related to the language barrier, not to anything else about Barbara and her ability to work with me or to relate to others. Once that relationship was established, we began to recognize and work with her individual difficulty in finding meaningful words to express emotions. With individuals for whom English is the mother tongue, we also must find a common language with our patients, so we can each understand, as clearly as possible (which is never completely), what the other means. We do this by attending to our internal reactions to our patients' remarks and to their reactions to our interventions, and by inquiring about reactions that seem incongruous or inconsistent. In all relationships, cultural issues will affect what we see as incongruous or inconsistent with our patient's life. Again, this element of the interaction with Barbara is more apparent, but not essentially different, than with English-speakers.

I am also somewhat less active, less ready to speak with Barbara than with others. I find if I follow the timing of "call and response" that I am used to, I often interrupt a comment from her as she pauses to think about how to understand what I said or how to say what she wants to say in English. So I wait longer to respond than my experience tells me is helpful. As I wait before speaking, I worry my silences will be experienced by her as lack of interest or unwillingness to be with her. Silences in Barbara's treatment are somewhat different in quality, as well as length, than in others. In my waiting to hear what more she has to add, I engage in the silent reverie that psychoanalysts learn to use: following my own associations to her thoughts, thinking about what her remarks mean in the context of what I know about her, thinking about what might be helpful to say. With native English-speakers, a long silence almost always means either anxiety or some important train of thought and I expect to address that. With English speakers, I usually have some sense of what the silence might mean. With Barbara, I am often not sure if her long silences are because she is uncomfortable with what I have said; if she is thoughtful about it; if she in fact understands what I have said; if she is still translating it to herself; if she is trying to translate what she wants to say back to me. Because I don't know, I don't know how to respond. My empathic understanding of our relationship, and of our exchanges, is disrupted by her need to translate back and forth. I find it is more important to be willing not to know, and to wait to find out about what Barbara is saying, than is sometimes the case. I also find if I am not attentive to my own emotional state, my waiting to find out can turn into disengaging from the interaction altogether.

Other therapists in the Chinese American Psychoanalytic Alliance (CAPA), which referred Barbara to me for treatment, experience the same disorienting difference in the verbal interchange, and it affects how we respond to our patients. Sometimes it affects even how we understand the level of emotional disturbance we may be working with. According to another colleague working in CAPA,

> often with my patient, I find myself clueless whether s/he actually understands what I've said, and at times wonder how disturbed s/he might be (briefly) because s/he'll respond in such a very different way to what I've said than seems to follow from what's happening. But so far these times seem to revolve around translation problems—a word, a tense. I, too, struggle to have a sense of whether I understand even the 'plain' meaning of what my patient says, never mind the associations, etc. Reverie is harder, because I feel myself straining at times to just understand 'simple' exchanges. . . . My patient talks about feeling s/he's a fake therapist and a fake person, and I feel I'm a fake person too, trying to offer depth therapy at such a distance in a language that's second to my patient's. (Cressida Forester, personal communication, 2010)

As I have noted, these issues are not peculiar to working with people for whom English is not the mother tongue. Another therapist involved with CAPA, Ralph Fishkin (2010, personal communication), believes, as I do, they are different only in intensity, not in fundamental nature, because of the language difference. Everyone we meet has their own internal world, different from ours, and we can never be completely sure that we have understood it fully.

I am always aware I may not understand exactly what my patients are saying, that there may be gaps in communication because of language, or idiom, or my inability to hear someone who speaks softly. As with Aaron, and with other people who speak very softly or very rapidly, I sometimes miss parts of what they say and must decide whether or not to ask them to repeat it. Sometimes I do not ask and wait to see if the ongoing conversation clarifies it; sometimes I feel I must ask in order to make sense of the ongoing conversation. Each of these choices affects how I perceive my patient and how I perceive our therapeutic work.

At times we believe we know what has been said, but are wrong. In my own psychotherapy, many years ago, I had an experience of such a mismatch between what was said and what was heard. I brought a dream about a feathered object and recounted it to my therapist. We talked for several minutes about various associations, which seemed relevant and useful to me, but after some minutes I had realized my therapist misunderstood "feathered" for "fetid." He assumed the dream was fairly negative and unpleasant for me, when in fact it was essentially neutral. Since I no longer remember what the dream was about, I cannot say why it took so long for me to realize the misunderstanding and to correct it, but the misunderstanding was in itself informative and suggestive: Informative about my over-compliance with my therapist's ideas; suggestive about the possibility that in a "neutral" dream were buried some negative thoughts or feelings that I could not acknowledge.

In order to recognize and be able to consider these subtle effects of the *form* of communication, over and above cognitive content, we must make a deliberate attempt to think about them. With Lily, I was not able to be clear about what happened in her therapy until I found a way to think clearly about her form of communication, after I managed to write about it. With Aaron, I knew for some time I was uncomfortable about our work together and I did not feel I was fully engaged in thinking about him and his life. I was unable to bring that awareness into my interaction with him and fully engage with him, until I realized how often I felt there were missing pieces in his conversation. That recognition allowed me to begin to ask about what was missing and to look at how his language reflected his life patterns.

Such a deliberate attempt to recognize the effect of word choice and speech patterns on our relationship is foreign to most of our everyday interactions with others. It is, however, a part of what makes doing psychotherapy, and learning to understand others who are different from us, simultaneously difficult and fascinating.

For the most part, I believe working with individuals whose first language is not English is different from working with native English speakers only in the clarity with which we recognize the issues. Even in working through translators, there are parallels to working with primarily English speakers. Translation between languages is quite problematic. Word-for-word translation is, almost always, at least a little misleading; but translation/ interpretation that involves the interpreter paraphrasing what is actually said can be misleading in other ways. The interpreter's own internal world shapes his or her perception of what the patient says, which in turn shapes what s/he chooses to tell the therapist: often the interpreter will say what s/he thinks the patient means, rather than what the patient has said. Only once have I felt that an interpreter-mediated interview was satisfactory. In that case, the interpreter confined himself to providing the semantic content of the patient's remarks, with occasional comments, clearly identified as his own, about social context and idioms in the patient's culture. In working with English speakers, where we assume we do not need a translator, we nevertheless must keep in mind what the patient means by a particular word may be different in small ways (or sometimes even in large ways) from what we mean by that word. Any time we find ourselves confused or surprised by a misunderstanding, we must ask ourselves if the problem relates to the patient using a different "language" than ours—a different idiom, or different meanings than we are used to.

At one point in my work with CAPA, one of the Chinese professionals I was supervised began providing psychotherapy to an American living in China, working in English as his first language but her second. We talked about her concerns about the language barrier and how many of the nuances of the communication she would miss. On one occasion, she told me she commented to her patient that he "liked" to do something, which in Chinese conversation means he does it often, he tends to do it, not that he enjoys it or he intentionally does it. He misunderstood her, thinking she meant he did it intentionally. He was able to come back for the next session and tell her he disagreed, allowing them to talk about the behavior in question and about the cultural issue in communication, as well as about the hazards of direct word-for-word translation, instead of context-driven translation (Ba Tong, personal communication, 2011).

Sometimes there are no words for what we want to say, and we must try to find words that will serve our purpose accurately. Another colleague involved in cross-language psychoanalytic and psychotherapeutic work is M. Hossein Etezady, in Philadelphia. Dr. Etezady is the head of the newly established Tehran Psychoanalytic Institute (TPI) in Iran, where they conduct all classes and supervision in Persian. Their reasoning was the language shift poses a barrier to emotionally-focused communication, and they hope to minimize those barriers. The Iranian professionals are very clear in their belief that psychoanalytic work without the emotional resonances of the "mother tongue" is insufficiently immediate and can miss the contextual significance as well as the personal meaning of the experience. Dr. Etezady, who moved to the United States as a young adult, commented on his struggles to use his "childhood" Persian to talk about very complex issues (Etezady personal communication, 2010). He believes it is difficult but important to find Persian words to reflect psychoanalytic concepts and the emotional connection to the language is an important element of that effort.

Finding language that accurately reflects our meaning is a task on the "macro" level, as in Dr. Etezady's work, to find or create Persian terms for specific technical concepts and, on the "micro" level, in our work every day with our patients and in our lives, finding words that say clearly what we intend. In every successful therapy, the patient and therapist together find ways to talk about the things that matter to the patient, finding ways to make words do what we need. As we work to understand what we hear from each other, and to find ways to say what we mean more clearly, we find ways to move closer to each other or to distance ourselves. In the next chapter, I describe some of the ways language allows us to bridge that interpersonal gap.

Chapter Four

Bridging the Gap

Language and Relational Distance

Our language allows us not only to reveal ourselves to others and to keep secrets from others; it allows us to make distinctions among the people whom we encounter in our everyday lives. As we live in the world of Others, finding the space we need in our relationships, we determine how we relate to those Others in part by our language. We all have different "languages" we speak with different people in our lives. We may use a sort of slang or idiom with close associates and a more formal and distancing vocabulary and syntax with business associates or strangers. Within our most intimate relationships, we can find clues to shifting levels of intimacy in our language. "Mommy," for instance, is generally for the mother/child relationship when the child feels dependent, with little autonomy, while "mother" is more often for the more mature individual, who expresses his differentness and distance from the mothering that makes him feel like a child. Even in this book, this phenomenon appears. I have consciously chosen to use a language (for the most part) that is accessible to interested laypersons, rather than the language that only psychoanalysts and psychotherapists can follow. In chapter 5, however, as I described the ways in which language develops, the language is somewhat "drier" and more distant, perhaps less immediately engaging, because it is about what I know, not what I have experienced.

As we work with our patients in psychotherapy, we can see how the choice of which language to use affects and is affected by their emotional functioning. Again, these issues can be examined more easily in examining language shift from English to other languages, than in examining language shift among the different groups in our lives.

My first encounter with thinking consciously about the emotional contributions of language choice was during my child psychiatric training, when an early supervisor reminisced about seeing someone in a language other than her childhood tongue (Maria Krocker-Tuscan, 1979, personal communication). This supervisor was born in Eastern Europe and left around the time of World War II. She spoke multiple languages. She remembered a time when she treated a patient—also polylingual—in Spanish and the patient brought a dream. As the two of them explored the dream, associations began to come in German rather than Spanish and the analyst followed without noticing the switch. Associations in German were significantly different than in Spanish and it was only in retrospect the analyst and the patient noted the shift and wondered about it. That neither noticed the shift of language suggests that Dr. Krocker-Tuskan was well-engaged in the patient's emotional world, following the different emotional resonances of the different languages without effort.

In "The Babel of the Unconscious," Amati-Mehler and his colleagues (Amati-Mehler, Argentieri, and Canestri, 1990) explore these issues at some length. They suggest that learning a second language after childhood offers opportunities for the individual to develop new affective experiences and new representations along with the new language, side-stepping unconscious conflicts associated with early childhood development and experiences and allowing new emotional adaptations to the world around them. New languages, they point out, may allow new social functions and be associated with different social status. Much of the early literature on this topic is from the 1950s, at a time when many European analysts and their patients relocated because of the war, and the losses and traumas associated with the need to learn new languages were often evoked in shifting language choices. In the twenty-first century, speaking English in non-English-speaking countries may allow access to educational or business opportunities that are otherwise not available, and political realities in the global economy often mean multilingual individuals can achieve goals that are otherwise quite difficult.

The language spoken may also maintain (or repudiate) an emotional tie with the parents from whom the "mother tongue" was learned. Amati-Mehler et al. present the striking case of a Spanish-born woman who, as an adult, was unable to speak Spanish when she started her analysis. She specifically chose an Italian analyst and then at several points in the analysis moved to speaking French without initially knowing whether her analyst spoke French. Later in the analysis, after her father died, the patient began to speak Spanish again, presumably because of internal psychological changes related both to her feelings about her father's death and to conflict resolution within the analysis. In these authors' words, the analysis "helped her to construct the interior paths through the languages toward integration and re-establishment of contact with conflictual and remote parts of the self; linguistic pathways re-establish the ties between the past and present, re-signifying and re-symbolizing the conflicts in retrospect" (p. 574).

Amati-Mehler also raised questions about what I refer to as the "emotional resonances" of words with the same content spoken in different languages, offering the example that the French word "fromage" evokes different internal images than does the English word "cheese." The related paths through sensorial memories—taste, smell, texture—and through emotional experiences connected with each are too specific and individual for the associative paths to be the same for everyone. In a therapeutic endeavor, which works through free association, then, the unconscious material accessed by the different languages must inevitably be at least somewhat different.

In this paper, Amati-Mehler and his colleagues make clear for us the ways language use in the polylingual (who have known more than one language from the early days of language acquisition) and the polyglot (who learned later languages as an adult) may reflect defensive adaptations. They present clinical cases of several individuals who were able to access parts of their internal emotional experiences only in one or another language. For the Spanish-born woman mentioned above and for others described, the second language allows for

> an emotional detachment from the words of the first-learned language, which preserves the whole load of emotional and perceptual experiences linked to early concrete bodily experiences, within those primary relationships during which the child, even before he can speak, learns the meaning of the words and the connexions between words and things—the "word-bath," as Spitz so aptly describes it . . . we believe that by substituting the childhood language with a new language which provides new paths for thoughts and affects, and by using a cultural and emotional context which is not marked by archaic conflicts, some patients not only submit to their resistances and defences, but are also able to create new pathways (even at the cost of deep and painful splittings) towards valid and structuring introjections. (p. 574)

Amati-Mehler et al. are quite clear it is not necessary for the analyst or therapist to speak multiple languages in order to assist the patient in resolving internal conflicts that are expressed in this way. It is, however, necessary for the therapist to remember the patient may use a second language in order to avoid confronting painful or frightening thoughts which can initially be thought only in the "mother tongue"; and it is necessary for the therapist to find ways to help the patient access the painful or frightening thoughts, with the important associated emotions, in the therapeutic work.

Krapf (1955) reports on his work in Argentina, where almost everyone speaks Spanish in everyday life, but the cosmopolitan nature of the country is so strong that many, if not most, residents speak several languages and it is commonplace for even native Argentinians to have conversations in French or English. He describes a patient who fled his mother country and his mother tongue in order to escape emotional domination by his mother and who spoke "an English of predominantly Latin origin. He avoided the strongly 'Saxon' vocabulary that British mothers and children ordinarily use with each other and spoke in a curiously stilted and 'affected' manner. This behavior changed in the course of his psychoanalysis . . . as his liberation from his castration anxiety allowed him to rediscover his tender feelings for his mother, his native tongue, and his mother country" (p. 346). As Krapf says, the use of one language or another by a patient serves always in some way to protect him from intolerable anxiety, either by altogether avoiding the emotional resonances inherent in the avoided language ("reinforcing repression") or by using terms that have weaker emotional resonances ("weakening the strength of a paralyzingly prohibitive superego") (p. 353).

In monolingual individuals, the shift is less often conscious or easily recognized. Many of us do not even think about the ways we shift our vocabulary according to listener or reader. Sometimes it is not vocabulary but prosody that shifts. My sister realized that when her son was an infant her Texas accent—which was largely lost by the time she had her baby—came back full force and her "mother tongue" was clearly that which she heard from her own mother. In my own case, although I have no children of my own, I have patients who require a maternal presence at times. In the last ten years, I have realized my own Texas accent, again largely lost after thirty years out of the state, returns in the form of drawling and dropping G's when I am with a very distressed and anxious patient. Again, the experience of being mothered and soothed returns within me and provides the model for how I can soothe and mother others who need that nurturance.

JARGON AND DIALECT AS DEFENSIVE ADAPTATIONS

We recapture the emotional resonance of speech by shifts in our language, including intonation and rhythm as well as vocabulary. We may also avoid the emotional resonances of our thoughts by couching them in more stilted, professional terms, jargon, or what I sometimes call "psychobabble." To say one has problems with anger management evokes very different feelings from saying "When I get mad I want to kill someone." A patient who talks about "anger issues" may, for long periods, avoid recognizing the loss of control inherent in his rage and, thus, avoid recognizing the fear of loss of control that lies under the rage.

In professional literature, using jargon—and abbreviations, which are increasingly common—also serves to distance both the writer and the reader from the emotions experienced within the therapeutic experience. For me, the abbreviation and the jargon each take a step back from the reality conveyed by the words in the term (e.g., PTSD as opposed to posttraumatic stress disorder) and the need to remember what the term refers to requires me to take a step back from my engrossment in the material I am reading.

Professionals with a common task and common training often develop particular terms that serve as a sort of shorthand for complicated thoughts, allowing us to communicate quickly and reasonably accurately. Within the common professional culture, the emotions associated with the concepts are usually not lost, although they are distanced to allow for more sober reflection. Too often, however, when we talk with professionals with different backgrounds, or with non-professionals, about our work, we continue to use the shorthand terms, the jargon of our fields. At those times it becomes a barrier to communication, rather than a quick and easy way to convey complicated thoughts, if used without due attention to how others understand the terms. When we use such jargon with our patients, it almost always interferes with clear communication. Not infrequently I see patients who will talk about their defenses, or their regression, or their "anger issues." My habit is to say I know what that phrase means to me, but I'm not sure what it means to them, and to ask them to say the same thing in other words. More often than not they are unable to do so, because they picked up the words from a previous professional encounter without a true understanding of the meaning.

Using jargon may, at times, facilitate thinking clearly about the work being described, but it may also interfere with applying what we read and learn to being in the room with a patient. Saying a child has ODD (oppositional defiant disorder) does not convey the level of irritation I may feel when every single thing I say or ask is met with anger, denial, and oppositional behavior, when the child's driving motivation is "You can't make me." If I want to work with that child, it is important for me to remember she is responding to her own "reading" of our relationship, that when I ask her how she feels about meeting with me, likely what she hears is something like, "You're crazy and bad and I'm going to make you change." No wonder she refuses to do what I ask! If I think of her as "the girl with ODD," however, it becomes immeasurably more difficult for me to remember how unhappy she likely is and, therefore, more difficult for me to develop any sort of emotional connection that will allow us to work together.

At its extreme, the use of jargon in writing may require a sort of translation as one reads, in order to be able to understand what is read. This of course interferes with applying what we read even in thinking about the patient. In reading the psychoanalytic literature, for instance, discussions of various forms of internalization require I hold in my mind the differences among internalization, identification, and introjection. These differences are important and can be described in several sentences each, but to read about them using those specific terms requires that I "translate" from my everyday English vocabulary to my psychoanalytic English vocabulary, which is not quite as fluid and easily accessible to my thought processes. I can do this in the privacy of my consulting room, or at home in the evenings, but in the room with a patient I am unable to do this and still be emotionally available to the interaction with the patient.

Using jargon may also serve as a screen for a lack of complete understanding. I would argue if one is unable to explain a professional concept in "everyday English"—even if it requires several sentences or even paragraphs to do so—then perhaps one does not truly understand the concept. Each shortcut of jargon represents a condensation or loss of meaning that compromises our ability to think clearly and accurately about the very complicated topics at hand. If we are unable to "unpack" those condensations, we lose information and distort our understanding. Some of the problems we encounter in communicating with professionals who have different theoretical viewpoints arise because we forget what they mean by a particular technical word may not be exactly what we mean by the same word.

Other information is encoded in the language we use. We all have multiple views of ourselves and others, and the way we speak to each other includes that information. Multilingualism may allow us to express some feelings more easily in, for instance, English than in Italian, but even the monolingual individual will have different vocabularies for different sorts of relationships. The different "languages" I refer to—what Amati-Mehler calls "baby language, love language, family vocabulary" (p. 580)—all offer us the opportunity to express various relational complexities without specific verbalization. Some languages have "intimate" and "formal" pronouns—e.g., French *tu* and *vous.* We may refer to the same person as *tu* at times, and at other times—perhaps when angry—as *vous.* Pronouns within all languages express "us" in opposition to "them," describing our relational distance. Even in languages where there are no clear ways to express distance or intimacy, the construction of our sentences and the vocabulary we choose is different. I speak differently with my sisters than I do with current close friends, and differently with those friends than with professional colleagues, and differently with those colleagues than with strangers.

Amati-Mehler et al. call this multilevel language choice "polydiscursive polylogism (co-presence in the mind of two or more discourses)" (p. 579). They state, in addition to the "co-presence of discourses" in a single language, the same linguistic discourse—the same words in the same order—can assume different meanings according to the emotional and relational context. For psychotherapists and psychoanalysts trying to parse our patient's communications, remembering the "co-presence of discourses," so we can listen from within both discourses, is crucial. If we are unable to keep in our mind that the patient's experience is different from our own and so what the patient means by a particular phrase or word may be different than what we would mean, we will miss important parts of what we need to know to be helpful. Our ability to "feel our way into" the patient's mind is what allows us to help our patients find ways to heal themselves. In order to "feel our way into" their mind, we must also feel our way into their language patterns and habits.

What Weinreich (quoted in Amati-Mehler et al., p. 571) called "linguistic contact"—the ways that one connects emotionally with others by the use of words—is a part of what I have called "relational distance." Every time we use a language, a dialect, a slang, or an idiom that our listener or reader does not know, we increase the relational distance and we reduce the amount of "linguistic contact" in our relationship. Every time we use a shared language, or a shared idiom, we reduce that distance and intensify the relationship.

In our interpersonal adaptations, we all try to find ways to be warmed by closeness without being consumed by the other, to maintain our independence and autonomy without being isolated and alone. The sum total of those interpersonal adaptations determines how we relate to others and how our personality style shows itself to those in the world around us. Language, with its unique characteristics allowing us to express simultaneous intimacy and separation, is a crucial part of this process.

THE DYADIC NATURE OF SPEAKING

Often we think of speech as committed by one person, without the input of anyone else. In fact, I would argue, speaking is a dyadic process: a listener, one is unable to speak. At any time that we form our thoughts into words, we have an audience, whether it be someone in the room with us or someone in our internal world, in our mind. When we speak, we attempt to build a bridge between ourselves and the other, finding ways to remind ourselves that we are not alone in the world. When we speak and are heard, we know that others exist in our world.

The fantasy of perfect communication is represented in the myth of the Tower of Babel, of a time when there was only one language and everyone understood. Despite this myth, perfect communication is never possible. Donnel Stern (DB Stern 2002, p. 242) and others (Pally 2001, Rizzuto 2003, Vivona 2003) argue that "words are always inadequate to the task they are set," that verbalizing an experience inevitably falsifies it. Stern says,

> As Freud held, the verbal and the nonverbal are incommensurable; once you grasp an experience in words, whatever it was before is gone: language changes what it formulates. But parting with Freud, for whom the unconscious meaning was the real, true one, a hermeneutic view leads us to the conclusion that what we formulate in words is not necessarily a degraded or diluted or

paler version of what it interprets, but a *different* meaning. Words create the
particular kind of meaning that can exist only in language. (p. 238)

Each time we formulate a sentence about our experience, we are trying to
find a way to allow the Other, our audience, to share some small part of our
experience. We try to create bridges to span the chasm that separates us from
others. Whenever we make ourselves like others or different from others
through our speech—using the same language, using a common idiom, using
a more personal pronoun or a more formal one—we are building those
bridges.

When our communication succeeds, we see the Other as not completely
alien, as like us in some ways, and so we feel closer and safer. When we
don't succeed in communicating clearly, we feel less close. In psychotherapeutic encounters, the ability to bridge the gap between patient and therapist
is an integral part of what makes the therapy run. Our patients tell us in
various ways that we have understood or not understood, that they feel (or
don't feel) "held" or "grounded" or "known." Many years ago one of my
patients, a professional musician, would bring in music for me, to communicate her feelings. When I had to tell her that the communication was not
successful, because music did not speak to me in the same way that it did to
her, she was afraid that I would never understand: to her, words felt meaningless, and she felt chronically alone and isolated.

Because we can never really know what the other person is thinking, but
can only approximate it, we must always strive to find ways to bridge the gap
in meaning between our mind and the mind of the other. Ogden (1994) tells
us that in psychoanalysis the patient learns to speak the analyst's tongue and
the analyst learns to speak that of the patient, as they co-create a space where
each understands the other as well as can be achieved, creating the "analytic
third." In his words from a later time (1997), psychoanalysis requires "the
development of metaphorical language adequate to the creation of sounds
and meanings that reflect what it feels like to think, feel, and physically
experience (in short to be alive as a human being to the extent that one is
capable) at a given moment" (p. 5). The analyst strives to "more fully cap-
ture/create his thoughts, feelings, perceptions, and so on in the analytic discourse" (p. 5). Note that Ogden does not say that the analyst *fully* captures his
thoughts and feelings, but that he strives to come closer to capturing them,
understanding that they can never be fully captured.

Ogden in fact knows that the lack of complete accuracy in reflecting
one's thoughts can be valuable, and he advocates practicing "the art of *not*
arriving [at specific meaning]" (Poirier, quoted in Ogden 1997, p. 3). Language, he argues, is not precise, and it is most useful exactly when it is
"dirty," when it simultaneously generates meaning and casts doubt on meaning. Freud recognized this capacity of words, and in *The Psychopathology of*

Everyday Life he discussed puns, slips of the tongue, and other ways that the unconscious makes use of the polysemic (having multiple meanings) nature of language.

For Ogden, the ambiguity of language perturbs by opening possibilities. When we want to avoid uncomfortable thoughts and feelings, we may want to avoid possibilities, to shut off alternative meanings to what we are saying. Then we speak in a constricted and constricting way, trying to be as specific as possible so as not to allow for ambiguity. We may think of the communicative third (by analogy with the analytic third, an experience created cooperatively between speaker and listener) as offering a space to be filled with meaning. The more specific we try to be, the more we fill the communicative space with our own meaning, and the less room we offer our listener to enter and to co-create a new experience.This new experience, shared between ourself and our listener, can offer new choices for responses to life.

As we speak with others and listen to others, we reach out to try to fill the communicative space with meaning, and bridge the gap between our own experience and that of others. Sometimes we finish sentences for others; sometimes we offer words, as when children don't have the vocabulary to tell us what they mean. When we offer our own thoughts or words to others, it may help them to find their own words. At other times it communicates falsely because we did not accurately grasp what they were trying to say. Aaron, in chapter 3, left things unsaid, so that I often felt that something was missing, that I needed to listen for another few sentences for the missing pieces. The missing pieces never appeared, however, and I have come to suspect that he omitted parts of his thoughts in the service of his own defensive structure: that if he had communicated clearly with me he would also have been required to know things himself that he wanted to avoid. If I had offered thoughts to fill in the missing pieces of his conversation, I might have made more sense of what he was saying; but it would have been *my* sense, not Aaron's sense, and so would have misled us.

When we offer our own thoughts and words to others, it may also communicate falsely because the words we use have "a long history of having served in interpersonal encounters in the past. Thus they arrive at the analytic hour wrapped up in feelings of other times and other scenarios of satisfaction, failure to communicate, hope or despair" (Rizzuto 2002, p. 1325). The history of *our* words is of necessity different from the history of the same words for our patient, and so what we say may not be what is heard. If you congratulate adolescents on good grades in school, what you likely mean is that you recognize their effort and their success at it. What some of them will hear is, "You don't have a life of your own, you have to obey adults and I'm glad about that." If we forget that what we say is not always what our communicative partner hears, our attempts to communicate and to work together will fail. The heart of psychoanalysis can often be found in the ways that our communications go awry, and what it tells us about the history of our patients' lives.

In a later paper (2003), Rizzuto tells us that "the patient's verbalization may mislead into believing that he is capable of fully engaging" (p. 1335) in affective communication. Many apparently articulate and intelligent individuals, however, use language to conceal the self rather than to reveal. Winnicott (1960) described "false self" individuals who have tried hard to please others and to hide themselves even from themselves, to the point of not being able to experience themselves as authentic. Rizzuto remarked in 2003 that in order for the patient to engage fully in the use of words to convey who he is, he must have experienced himself as an agent, as the "I" who feels and thinks and acts. Individuals who have not fully experienced the "I" in that way may use words more to hide, to pretend to be an agent, rather than to reveal themselves.

For Kay, when she entered treatment with me, her words allowed her to hide for much of the first eighteen months of her treatment, while still allowing her enough emotional sustenance from our relationship that she could keep functioning. When her internal emptiness became more intense and painful, the words and the relationship which they carried, began to fail and her depression worsened so much that we finally resorted to something other than words.

Vivona (2006) cites Daniel Stern, who asserts that language creates a chasm between verbal and nonverbal experiences; but Vivona believes that verbal experience supplements, rather than supplanting, nonverbal experience. Daniel Stern et al. (1998) and Vivona both appear to use "nonverbal experience" to refer to experiences that have not been, and perhaps cannot be, expressed clearly in words; Stern uses the term "implicit relational knowing" (p. 903) to refer to such experiences, and is quite clear that such knowing can persist throughout life. Vivona believes that with growth and development nonverbal experience becomes secondary to verbal experience, and that it can contradict and confuse our verbal understandings of our world. She believes that language can nevertheless be used to understand, reconsider, and organize our experience, offering connections to "lived experience"—the nonverbal domain of our experience—and allowing us to use our language to change what that experience means to us and how it shapes our lives. This, of course, describes at least one aspect of what psychotherapy accomplishes: we use language to help our patients understand their past history and current experience, and to make new meanings for themselves out of what they understand.

Neither Stern nor Vivona has completely described the relationship between lived experience and how we verbalize it. Certainly there is lived experience that cannot be put into words clearly; and implicit knowledge that simply exists without thinking about it in words (how often do you think about how to walk?). Certainly also, when we begin to talk about our experience, to some extent the memory of the experience within us changes as we use words to capture and hold onto it. However, it is not my experience that nonverbal experience becomes secondary to verbal experience, even when we spend many hours trying to find words for it. Instead I would borrow Amati-Mehler's words and refer to a "co-presence of discourses." We have an internal verbal discourse, which uses words to capture some parts of the experience, however incompletely. The internal verbal discourse lives side-by-side with the internal nonverbal discourse that is the emotional and visceral memory. We use the verbal discourse to communicate parts of our experience to others, because sometimes it is the only way we have to share profound visceral experiences; but I do not believe that we lose the nonverbal internal discourse only because we have found words for some part of the experience. It is because we know there is more to share that poets, authors, painters, and musicians persist in trying to find ways to capture and convey to others that internal visceral experience.

Each way of knowing affects the other.Even as finding words for an experience shapes the memory of the experience, the inability to find those words, to convey fully what we are feeling, acts as a stimulus to emotional development and growth. Donald Winnicott, who described so many of the things about children that we did not have words for before his words, has talked about the importance of "not knowing" what the other is saying to us. As he discusses his "Theory of the Parent-Infant Relationship" (1960), he reminds us that "infant" implies not talking, suggesting that "it is not un-useful to think of infancy as the phase prior to word presentation and the use of word symbols. The corollary is that it refers to a phase in which the infant depends on maternal care that is based on maternal empathy rather than on understanding of what is or could be verbally expressed" (p. 587).

He goes on to describe the early days of life, in which the closer mother can come to understanding the infant's needs fully, the better. However, as the infant begins to walk, to soothe himself, and to begin to exert his will on the external world, a change begins. Then Winnicott says, mother also changes, and

> It is as if she now realizes that the infant no longer expects the condition in which there is an almost magical understanding of need. The mother seems to know that the infant has a new capacity, that of giving a signal so that she can be guided towards meeting the infant's needs. It could be said that if now she knows too well what the infant needs, this is magic and forms no basis for an object relationship.
>
> In other words, at the end of merging, when the child has become separate from the environment, an important feature is that the infant has to give a signal. (p. 593)

This is one of the life changes that drives the development of language, as the child learns to signal his needs.

In psychotherapy and psychoanalysis, as is so often the case, there are parallels between the child's early development and events within the therapeutic hour. We work hard to understand our patients, both what they are telling us and what they are unable to tell us. However, as with the infant, if we always know without being told, "this is magic and forms no basis for an object relationship" (Winnicott 1960, p. 592). Our ultimate goal is for the patient to be able to articulate what he feels and needs and wants, to himself and for others when he chooses. In order to help him reach this goal, it is very important

> that the analyst shall *not* know the answers except in so far as the patient gives the clues. The analyst gathers the clues and makes the interpretations, and it often happens that patients fail to give the clues, making certain thereby that the analyst can do nothing. This limitation of the analyst's power is important to the patient, just as the analyst's power is important, represented by the interpretation that is right and that is made at the right moment, and that is based on the clues and the unconscious co-operation of the patient who is supplying the material which builds up and justifies the interpretation. . . . The analyst may appear to be very clever, and the patient may express admiration, but in the end the correct interpretation is a trauma, which the patient has to reject, because it is not his. (Winnicott, 1960, p. 592)

It is in our not-knowing, our embrace of the failure of language and of words, that we foster autonomy over emotional dependence, that we help our patients to be able to go out of the consulting room into the outside world and manage for themselves what we have been doing for and with them in the treatment.

Chapter Five

Normal Language Development

As humans, we are specialized to live in a social environment. Our ability to be social is what allows us to join with others to gather food, to raise animals for food, to farm, to live in groups. Ultimately, our ability to be social is what led to civilization, to industrialization, and to commerce. Our brain is "designed" to manage social interactions (Pally, 2011, personal communication) and those social interactions enable us to survive, to thrive, and to accomplish most of the things we accomplish either singly or in groups. Susan and Kay show us some of the ways language helps us as individuals to live in our social environment and some of the ways this can go wrong.

While we are learning to speak to others and to ourselves, we are also learning to manage our feelings; to remember others; to remember thoughts and feelings; to influence others to assist us in accomplishing things we cannot do alone; to think about what might happen and plan to change what is happening; to fit in with groups of others by how we speak; and in general to do all the things that allow us to function as adults in a complicated world. All of these achievements use language in complex ways that take place, for the most part, outside our conscious awareness. We develop our language and our ability to use it in these complex ways, in the first several years of life, at the same time we are learning to walk, to manage our bodies, and to manipulate objects, along with many other capacities we use as adults. Susan showed us some of the ways early developmental problems can interfere with language acquisition and use. Kay, who had apparently normal language acquisition, nevertheless had problems in the way she was able to use language (to talk about and identify emotions), because of problems in early relationships, in the years when she was developing her language.

In this chapter, I describe the developmental line of language: the way it develops from birth to perhaps five years, when it is essentially fully developed except for vocabulary. As we go along, I point out various steps with a direct impact on the development of capacities that become important later in life. In the next chapter, we look at some of the ways development can go astray.

While thinking about these events in the life of the baby, we should remember, as Winnicott (1960) said, there is no baby without a mother: the baby's development is inextricably tied to and dependent upon how his mother manages him. We should also remember that describing average expectable, "normal" development cannot be used inflexibly to describe every single baby. Rather, what you read here is a close approximation of what most families see in their babies. Throughout the book, I use "he" and "she" interchangeably to indicate babies and other individuals of either gender. I also use "mother" as shorthand referring to the baby's primary nurturing figure. We should remember, however, not all caretakers are mothers or even women, and babies can be girls as well as boys.

In 1981, Rose Edgcumbe described the developmental line of language acquisition, beginning with the first days of life. This developmental line is, of course, closely synchronized with early child development and any description of language acquisition reflects that synchrony. Reading her description of language development, we begin to recognize that many of the things we see in and do with our infants in the first months of life in fact play a role in their language development. She identified various stages in acquiring language that help us examine more closely the different interpersonal and intrapersonal skills the baby develops.

The first three stages Edgcumbe describes occur very quickly, almost simultaneously, in the first six months of life. They describe the baby's move from formless, biologically driven noises such as crying when hungry or uncomfortable, toward the intentional use of sounds, which are not yet words, as in babbling. The next three stages are concerned with the different uses of established sounds and the intentional use of something that is recognizably language, as opposed to non-word sounds. In these later stages, the baby's aim-directed behavior replaces his biologically determined behavior: so instead of aimless arm-waving he will reach for a desired object; instead of crying out of hunger he will make noises he knows will bring mother; and eventually he will say mama.

Edgcumbe began with birth, but today we know the baby's relationship to aural communication—to language—begins even earlier. Even *in utero*, infant heart rates increase when mother reads a poem and decrease when a female stranger reads the same poem (Kisilevsky et al. 2003).

Newborns are able to control the frequency with which they suck on a pacifier and can learn a "high amplitude" suck causes the presentation of a stimulus. They also look toward the source of a sound as they listen and can be taught that turning toward a particular stimulus will lead to a "speech sample." Using these and other behavioral responses from infants, researchers can make observations and draw conclusion about the capacities of the infants (Vivona, 2012). Such research teaches us that the capacity to perceive and process speech sounds is present before birth and develops quickly over the first weeks of life (Kisilevsky et al., 2003). At less than a week of age, newborns demonstrate a behavioral preference for human speech over similar complex sounds (Vouloumanos and Werker, 2007). This preference for speech assists the infant in attuning to the speech of others and facilitates the process of learning to understand the meaning of the sounds (Vivona, 2012) mother makes as she tends him.

In addition to discriminating speech from non-speech sounds, newborn infants are able to discriminate the phonemes (basic meaningful speech sounds) present in all human languages and can remember the acoustical patterns and rhythms of speech. At less than three days of age, babies respond differently to passages their mothers read aloud twice daily in the final six weeks of the pregnancy than they do to unfamiliar passages (DeCasper and Spence, 1986). It seems clear the infant's ability to perceive speech as distinct from other sounds begins even before birth, and newborns can identify the rhythmic and acoustic patterns of speech even when not in mother's familiar voice. Thus, it is speech itself, and not mother's voice, they recognize. At only a few days, they are able to differentiate stress patterns and phonological characteristics of "content words," such as nouns, from those of "function words" indicating grammatical structure, such as "the" or "his" (Shi, Werker, and Morgan, 1999). Recognizing these speech patterns also is a precursor to true speech comprehension (Vivona, 2012).

At birth, when the baby exhibits physical distress and cries, mother responds *as if* the baby is communicating. When she reacts by feeding or changing or comforting her baby, usually she also talks to her baby, using, of course, the rhythms and patterns of speech. Although the baby's sounds are still meaning-free and arise from either reactions to physical sensations or from inbuilt biological mechanisms, mother's sounds are not. She responds as if the baby is letting her know he is hungry or wet or hurting, and when she tends to her baby her actions build the emotional connection between them. The repeated experience of hearing language also strengthens the infant's capacities to perceive speech, teaching the baby that sounds can have meaning. All speech patterns gain significance because they are uttered in activities and practices with another person for whom they already have significance. Those activities include feeding, bathing, playing, regulating affect states, and directing attention, but—significantly—not teaching language. Speech and other sign systems (such as gestures, body movements, facial expressions, songs) are simply part of these activities (Litowitz, 2012).

In the course of the feeding, bathing, playing, regulating affect states, and other activities of the baby-with-mother, the baby quickly learns to listen to and to watch mother's mouth, taking in her sounds, while the mother is learning to listen to and observe the baby's behavior, learning how his cry is different from those of other babies and how his various cries differ from each other. Because mother initially treated the baby's cries *as if* they are communication, they have begun to be communication in fact fairly early on. In Vivona's words (2012),

> Current research depicts an infant who is actively oriented to speech from the beginning of life and whose competencies to understand that speech, including its meanings, develop early and rapidly. We discover in this research a young infant who not only understands something of the meaning of the speech she hears, but who also uses that speech to organize both her perception and her conceptualization of the world, perhaps beginning as early as three months of age, with the perceptual and conceptual processes informing, as well as sometimes competing with, one another. . . . These capacities . . . emerge during the first year of life, before language acquisition proper. . . . Aural speech, when present, affects how infants process the world, especially when that speech is part of an interaction with another person. (p. 255)

As the baby continues to grow, his early ability to differentiate speech sounds from other sounds grows and the rhythms and prosody of his native language are reinforced. Fairly quickly, he learns the features of vocal sounds that highlight meaning in his native language, and he learns not to attend to nonmeaningful vocal noises: by about eight months, phonemes not used in the native language are no longer perceived as linguistic signals (Litowitz 2011, Vivona 2012). This aspect of meaning is available to the infant long before the use of words as labels for objects or actions. As the baby learns the prosody of his mother tongue, he also develops a "receptive vocabulary" of sounds related to specific inner experiences. He recognizes emotional tones and can differentiate approving from disapproving affect in both familiar and unfamiliar languages (Fernald, 1993). Within weeks, he seems to have learned that a specific series of sounds in response to his hungry cry means he soon will not be hungry. He remembers what happened before when he felt the same sensations and made the same sounds, and his memory of past experience helps him to learn to wait a few seconds or even a few minutes for his feeding before his cry intensifies. This is an early form of the capacity to anticipate, and lets us know the baby is just beginning to create his own representational world, internal memories, and models of the world outside his body as he lives in and responds to that world.

As early as two months, the baby is not only receiving but producing vocal noises to engage others. We can observe vocal play with mother that sounds like conversation with adults (Trevarthen and Grant, 1979), and the babbling of the infant has taken on the prosody of the language in his home. German babies babble in German, Japanese babies babble in Japanese, and the rhythms and music of the babble mimic the rhythms and music of the mother tongue. In this vocal play, the babbling baby discovers the relational capacities of sounds made with his mouth, a foundation tool of language. "The tools that language provides create and mark changes in the relationships between self and others even as they bind us intrapsychically to one another" (Litowitz, 2012, p. 271).

By three months, the baby's first steps in primitive remembering and organizing of his experience make it possible for him to link his own sounds with specific inner experiences. He has already shown a preference for mother and for mother's voice, as he smiles at her face and voice but not at the faces or voices of others. He also begins to show, with smiles, coos, and excited movements—an "expressive vocabulary"—that he recognizes mother's preparations to feed him, bathe him, and so forth. When distressed, unless utterly overwhelmed and screaming, he will quiet to the sound of mother's voice even before she touches him.

We can now recognize that the baby experiences some differentiation of inner feelings, as the noises that accompany his pleasure can be distinguished from the noises that accompany his discomfort or unpleasure. Increasingly, the baby's vocal noises begin to occur along with actions, not only randomly. Tension discharge, a response to internal physical sensations, is still an important stimulus for some noises and gestures, but not all. Some are in response to mother's noises and gestures in another move toward relational communication.

As the child learns the sounds mother makes are somewhat predictable and attached to specific events, he also begins making his own patterned sounds. Mother's interaction with the baby initially includes communicative babbling, establishing the reciprocal noises that precede true language. It teaches the child some of the relational aspects of verbal communication: turn-taking, attending to the other's vocal productions, sharing a focus of attention with the communicative partner. He learns to follow the gaze of the other and to direct his own attention where the partner—mother—is attending. Toward the end of the first year the baby begins to understand others are acting in planful ways, and to appreciate the speaking adult has something to communicate (Vivona, 2012). He is able to distinguish communicative from noncommunicative behaviors (Yoon, Johnson, and Csibra, 2008) and to recognize that gestures, speech, tone of voice, and other elements of language are indicators of the intent to communicate. He also begins to understand what others are trying to communicate. By twelve to fourteen months he begins to use intentional gestures of his own (Liebal, Behne, Carpenter, and Tomasello, 2009; Liszkowski, Carpenter, and Tomasello, 2008; Tomasello and Rakoczy, 2003) as part of his own efforts to connect with others and to communicate.

As the child vocalizes and mother responds, her emotional support of the baby is available from a distance because baby recognizes her voice. Winnicott (1960) called this emotional support "holding," meaning not only physical holding but also emotional holding and regulation of the baby's emotions. When the baby can recognize mother both visually and vocally, he can know mother is present even when not close by, because he can see her across the room and hear her when she is not visible. With his growing awareness that mother's sounds mean food or some other comfort is imminent, he begins to form and maintain at least a brief internal image of mother. He has learned how it feels to be safe with mother and now he is learning to recreate that experience within his own developing self, with less reference to mother's external capacities and contributions. Now he can sustain for a few seconds a sense of "safe harbor" within the mother-child dyad. These are the earliest seeds of a capacity for self-regulation, which in adulthood allows us to maintain ourselves emotionally.

Even in the first days of life, in the average expectable family, mother thinks about her baby as an Other, a different person who can recognize and love her. This helps her to stay (mostly) calm and positive about herself as mother and to be calm and positive about her baby. As she tends her baby, she often maintains a running commentary about her perceptions of him. This strengthens her connection with the baby and helps her to stay attuned as she thinks about what he might be feeling: "Oh, you're crying! Are you hungry? But I just fed you, so maybe something else is upsetting you." Because she is talking to and about him as separate and different from her, this running commentary helps her to remember he is an independent person; mother's perception of the child as independent helps the child to learn to perceive himself as someone who is not exactly like mother, but who feels differently even when he does not have the words for that experience. Just as mother's treating the newborn's cry *as if* it were communication helped to turn his cries into communication, mother's treating the months-old infant *as if* he has an existence separate and autonomous from her helps to make him in fact separate and at least potentially autonomous in his own mind as well as in physical reality. When mother recognizes the baby's separateness, consistently tends his physical needs, and helps regulate his distress, he begins to develop a primitive sense of a self that *can* be regulated.

By the middle of the first year, research suggests (Vivona, 2012) the infant is able to process mother's stream of speech and discern discrete words. Many infants begin to understand at least some words in the second half of the first year of life. The first words understood usually are words with strong personal relevance: the child's own name, some version of "mama" or "dada." There is some research evidence that even words such as "hand" and "foot" or words for familiar foods are recognized by six to nine months (Vivona, 2012). It is not clear how much of this recognition is related to the *linguistic* content of the words and how much to the *paralinguistic* information conveyed by prosody, accompanying gestures, vision, touch, taste, and so on. We do know (Singh, 2008) in the second half of the first year infants begin to recognize words independent of the tone used. Even prior to the second six months of life, they are "beginning to develop the foundational capacities that will enable them to use the linguistic information in the flow of speech directed to them" (Bucci, 2012, p. 279).

While mother talks to the child about what they both are doing, the child learns vocabulary as well as cause-and-effect. As he learns to understand what mother is saying, he begins to recognize that some things happen when they are not wanted ("Oops, I dropped your milk!"). Mother's reflection on the child's inner world ("Oh, you're crying, you're really sad") fosters his ability to reflect on himself. He is learning to observe himself as mother has observed him. This lets him more easily regain the memory of a "safe harbor" with mother and strengthens his capacity for self-regulation. As he learns to observe himself, he can more easily think about the world without acting on it and can recognize external events that do not involve him. He can then use his reflective capacity to try out new coping mechanisms, to understand what has happened outside himself, and to maintain a growing sense of mastery and competence.

Language supports the process of understanding how the world works through naming, labeling, and categorizing. The child learns to create categories of words that allow him to generalize to novel situations: knowing what a ball is allows a child to know more quickly that a new, unfamiliar ball can be played with in the same way as his old, familiar ball. He also learns to put his new experiences into words, and needs mother to help him reorganize his previous experiences and models of the world. For instance, mother may tell him that the unfamiliar (and scary) new car is "just like" the old familiar (and safe) car he knows, allowing him to locate the category "car" to help him understand his world and to manage his anxiety about new situations. By the middle of the first year, words serve as labels for existing concepts, but also help the infant to construct new concepts. Labeling two objects with the same word may help the infant to notice the similarities, as well as provoke him to ignore some ways in which he might otherwise discriminate the objects. He may have separated out several red toys as similar; but when they are labeled for him, he may be able to separate out the red and blue and yellow balls as *more* similar, leaving the red block and the red stuffed animal to be sorted in some other way.

As the infant learns to observe both objects and events and to predict events such as a ball falling when you let go of it, he also learns he can have an impact on the world around him. He can control where the ball falls; he may be able to throw the ball. When mother comments that he dropped the ball, he learns how to think about what happened and can then think about how he wanted, or how he wants, to have an impact on the world around him.

Words "invite infants to share in the wider world and to think about that world in new ways" (Vivona, 2012, p. 245), and verbal skills enhance our capacity to deal with the wider world. The more we are able to think about ourselves in the context of the world, the better we are able to maintain a sense of being OK even though we cannot control events around us. When mother explains and predicts events such as separation, and then predicts reunion (as when she leaves the child with a sitter but says she will be back), it is more tolerable to be left, because the child can use mother's words to remember she still exists and will be there again. The baby's new ability to call or cry and have mother come also helps the baby to know he has some minimal control over the world, that although mother goes away sometimes he can "make" her come back again. As Litowitz (2011) tells us, "expressing desires and getting others to do something are basic to all communicational exchanges. . . . (B)efore one is aware of what is being said . . . communicational exchanges are attempts to accomplish something," and expressing desires ("Want!") and getting something done ("Mama! Milk!") are the earliest of those attempts to accomplish some goal. When the child can "make" mother come back, it is slightly less distressing for him that mother sometimes leaves, as he remembers he is not totally helpless. His very early sense of agency in response to this new skill, and his concomitant progress in learning to crawl or walk, feeds a burgeoning autonomy, and he begins to understand himself as a separate being who has some impact on outside events.

When mother and child talk together about the toddler's inner world, they share a joint focus of attention. Through the shared attention and meaning they strengthen their emotional union (DN Stern, 1985). Again, however, the very existence of union implies the possibility of its absence, and language can serve as a contradiction to wishes for magical union through the possibility of being misunderstood. Naming emotional states and describing the child's inner state to him helps him to know his own mind and (later) to think about mother's. It helps to recognize both the ways mother's mind is similar to his and the ways mother's mind is different from his. The back and forth of union and separation through language within the relationship echoes the back and forth of union and separation through physical movement, and reinforces the growth of psychic structure and capacity to tolerate separation from mother.

By about five months, the infant establishes object permanence, the awareness that something (or someone) exists even when you cannot see it. The baby realizes noises—specifically vocalizing, noises made by others— can have particular meanings, and those noises can be used to influence the behavior of others. Edgcumbe (1981) believes that by this time the baby "has a primitive image of 'mother' whose attention he wants, and enough language organization to select appropriate sounds to attract her" (p. 77). He has the first seeds of understanding facial expressions, tries to imitate mother's vocal sounds, and enjoys repetitious naming of things, parts of the body, etc. For the child, perhaps imitating mother's vocal sounds represents an attempt to "become" mother—an early internalization (psychological appropriation of the function) of the mother who can do all the things the baby cannot do for himself.

At six months, the baby shows some evidence of responding differentially to different emotional tones of mother's voices, suggesting the early capacity to recognize that others have internal feelings different from his (what Fonagy has called "mentalization") (Fonagy et al., 2005). Over the next months, he begins to recognize his noises attract attention from others and some sounds have specific meaning. The games we play with our babies around this age include repetitious and pleasure-filled naming of parts of the body and of things. Shared pleasure in the game, in communication and specifically in language, strengthens the emotional bond between mother and child. It also gives the baby another reason to learn what the words mean, to please the person who is so important in his life. As mother and baby find the baby's nose, ears, and fingers together, they reinforce the baby's awareness of meaning, in the repetitive experience of naming the nose while touching the baby's nose. When we name a nose and touch our own nose, we also show the baby that words refer to *categories* of things, that there can be more than one nose: "nose" means not only "baby's nose," but "this thing on a face."

Between nine and twelve months, the baby's babbling reaches a peak and long babbled sentences continue even after the first recognizable words appear. In peekaboo and "drop and pick up" games, the baby learns some of the skills that accompany interactive speech: turn taking (e.g., something has to be dropped before it can be picked up), making and breaking eye contact, coordination of signaling and acting, development of facial expressions and gestures, and the principle that facial expressions may occur in response to gestures or noises. Adults playing with babies tend to use exaggerated expressions and reactions as we instinctively enhance this communicative property of interactions with them.

Previously the child has worked to adapt to and to adapt within the mother-child dyad, learning to do what mother wants (e.g., hold still to be diapered, or holding the bottle for himself). Now he must work consciously to make the world suit him, and he uses language to get mother to care for him. A part of his growing mastery of the world is the ability to say "want" to the primary caretaker and to have the "want" satisfied. Spitz' third psychic organizer (1965), the word "No," is another step toward mastery of the external world. It emphasizes mother and child are separate, and in that separateness the child can be comfortable and OK. When the mother-child unity is re-established after the "no," in the recurring to and fro of that dyad, "no" becomes again an experience of disunity that can be repaired and so the disunity is less disturbing.

By twelve months, early separation-individuation is well advanced, and hearing allows the infant to maintain contact with his mother through her voice even when she is not visible. Hearing offers advantages over sight as the baby enters the practicing phase of development, when he begins to explore the world more actively. When he can hear mother in the next room, he can know she is there, preventing the anxiety that comes with premature separation. He can call to mother and be answered, maintaining a psychological link through the language shared with mother. And he can cry to bring mother from the next room, exerting some control over the length of the separation. Crying to bring feeding or physical care, and noises to bring mother, are the very earliest steps as the baby begins to take some control over his environment, and they mark the beginning of individuation, the development of a sense of identity as a unique individual.

With the advent of intentional use of sounds, the infant is ready to move to developing different uses for established sounds. Behaviors begin to have psychological aims, determined now by biological needs such as hunger as well as by emotions and thoughts, as when the toddler wants mother's attention. This begins the second set of three stages in Edgcumbe's description (1981), with the acquisition of meaning for sounds understood before perhaps only by mother. Where mother could recognize a "hungry cry" from a "wet cry" from a "hurting cry," others who know the child only slightly may now also be able to recognize some of the communications.

By this time, the infant has discovered vocalization can influence others to do things and he "moves from using his own idiosyncratic sounds to learning the language conventions of his family" (Edgcumbe, 1981, p. 88). Words can now be used to express wishes, along with the previous nonspecific noises, which released impulses and affect. Words also help the child learn how to differentiate feelings and experiences (sad, angry, afraid as different types of unpleasure, for instance) and diverse relational objects (mother, father, sister). Because receptive speech always precedes expressive speech by about three months, children always understand what is said to them before they learn how to say what they mean. Perhaps, when he listens, the child can use contextual clues to find the meaning, but to speak he must summon up the correct word from his own internalized knowledge. Eventually, however, the first expressive words appear—perhaps mama, perhaps no—and the family's delight in the baby's speech reinforces his own delight in his accomplishment and his ability to have an impact on his world.

Around this time, words begin to serve as explanation and reassurance when used by mother, with the words as well as the soothing tone being reassuring. The child can recognize commands and prohibitions in the adult's words when they are spoken in a commanding or angry tone. As the commands and prohibitions are internalized and made a part of the child's self, the early seeds of superego and conscience formation are sown. The child internalizes both the caring and the controlling aspects of the important other person. Now he can remember mother's words and tones and can use this memory to call up the memory of her presence, to summon the internal experience of dwelling in the mother-infant dyad, along with whatever safety or comfort that experience carries for him. The child can also summon the memory of mother saying no and use that to stop the prohibited behavior, so as to keep alive the positive memory of approval in place of the negative memory of her anger or dismay. He is no longer totally dependent on mother's actual physical presence to experience the feeling of the safe harbor, and so the process of learning to be a separate distinct individual (separation-individuation) moves forward.

By twelve months, the child understands a few familiar words in context and comprehends and obeys simple commands when accompanied by gestures. He has learned mother and others are more pleasant when he obeys the simple commands. Perhaps things happen that he doesn't like, such as being carried away, or a swat on his rear, when he does not obey the simple commands. He is learning the sounds made by others have an impact on him and is learning his own sounds can have an impact on others.

As language grows and the child learns to think about himself, the need for pronouns appears. The first pronouns to appear (Owens, 2008) are generally "I" and "it," reflecting the nascent sense of identity, the self demarcated from the rest of the world. A few months later we hear "my" or "mine" and "you," with the recognition that things can be grouped ("mine") and of the self-ness of others ("you"). "You" helps the child to recognize that the Other is a person like him, with an internal world both like and unlike his own; that others have emotional lives; and that behavior has meaning connected to that emotional life. With the advent of pronouns, the child enters into

a relationship between self and other that is unique. Consider that the speaker is also always her own listener, no matter to whom her speech is addressed. In contrast, visual recognition of others does not include looking at the self who is also looking. Therefore, to look is to objectify, while speaking and hearing ineluctably entail intersubjectivity. From birth there is an entanglement between the one vocalizing and the one who hears the vocalizations, between oneself *for* another and oneself *as* another. . . . That doubled entanglement creates a unique self-other relationship that is instantiated in the very features of the language itself: namely, in the reversibility of the speaker ("I") and addressee ("you") discursive positions; and in the capacities for self-reference

(reflexivity) and recursiveness that are unique to linguistic systems." (Litowitz, 2011)

Interestingly, "we" and "s/he" occur at the same time, both slightly later than
"you." This reflects the child's ability to recognize that "you" and "I" each
have separate relationships to "her," which is different from the simple recognition that "you" and "I" exist. "We" asserts the belonging-together of
"you" and "I," and "s/he" asserts there is a third person outside that belong-
ingness. "S/he" is outside "I" as well as outside "you," and the world of
people is becoming complicated. This recognition of "s/he" tends to occur
around thirty to thirty-four months and is the first evidence of an emerging
recognition that there can be relationships with two other people, with "I"
competing with "you" for attention from "him." The ability to resolve this
relational conflict and to be comfortable in triadic relationships, to share
important lives with others in their lives, is a significant interpersonal
achievement, which allows living in groups.

The need for plural and singular pronouns strengthens the recognition of
separateness from others, as well as the possibility of "me" and "you" coming together as "us." The wish for "us" to prevail over "you two" in the
triadic competition gives special impetus to the meaning of "us" for the child.
Pronouns also reflect the child's recognition of people outside the dyad and
outside the family circle, as he learns "them." When these terms are added to
the developing vocabulary of the child, his internal representations of the
world and of relationships are reorganized. We begin to expect more emphasis on verbal "thinking about" and less on action as the way to consider what
is outside oneself and how to deal with the world. With verbal skills, early
secondary process (logic, and decisions that are less emotionally driven)
grows stronger, offering even more ways of coping with relationships and
with the world outside.

The reorganization of the baby's representation of the world and of relationships with others also includes what Fonagy has called "mentalization"
(Fonagy et al., 2005), the ability to understand and consider the point of view
of the other in an interaction. Recognizing that "s/he" is both not-me and not-
you implies recognizing that your view of her may be different from my view
of her. In addition, conversations with others make it clear that others have
different knowledge and beliefs than the child does and he learns to take
those differences into account in his communication. When I was a young
child, speaking Spanish to our family's Hispanic housekeeper, I knew that I
needed to speak English to my parents, but that Spanish was acceptable with
Hilda. I did not realize that they were two separate languages, but I certainly
knew who would understand which words best.

At around fifteen months, the baby can stop his own actions with his own
words, saying "no, no," even though he likely still requires the presence of an

adult to reinforce the no. He is beginning to develop the beginnings of a superego, a conscience to tell him that a particular behavior is bad or good. He is using a few recognizable words of his own, and understands many more. The use of sound to communicate has been replaced by the use of words to communicate, and the development of vocabulary is most likely picking up speed.

At eighteen months, the child is now a toddler, walking more or less freely, exploring the world. His enhanced ability to move physically away from mother requires him to use his progress in separation-individuation (awareness of himself as separate and distinct from mother) and object constancy (knowing that mother exists and still loves him even when not physically present) to be comfortable as he does so. Being able to talk to mother, to call her, to hear her when he is in another room, strengthens his ability to go out and explore without becoming frightened, and then return to the "safe harbor" of mother's arms. Because he is walking, he has many more objects in his life to look at and name and likely is in fact naming them as he points at them. His cognitive awareness of the world around him, including people and animals and the noises they make, is growing exponentially. He will echo the words of others at times, and tries to sing and join in nursery rhymes with others. By twenty-four months, most children will have dozens of recognizable words (at least recognizable by mother, if not by others), and will be able to form one to two word sentences.

Let me pause here to say again that not all children match this descriptive path of development. In general, we can name points along the way to orient ourselves in the overall developmental arc, but there is too much going on to describe early child development at all clearly. Most often, when we try to describe what we observe in a toddler, we choose one element to focus on, such as language, or walking, or physical dexterity. As we describe the growth of that part of the child's capacities, we refer to others; but to describe all the elements of development accurately would require being able to say multiple things all at once, and thus would be neither clear nor coherent.

By approximately twenty-four months, the child who is developing well will have object constancy well enough established to allow him to summon up the internal representation, the memory with associated emotions, of important people for purely internal reasons: he will be able to remember mother simply because he wants to, not only in response to the sound of her voice or a need for her. This allows him to use words linked with mental representations, such as "Mama," to reassure himself, and to reinforce mother's demands and prohibitions, even when mother is not physically present. He can use her familiar phrases to evoke the memory of her caring and controlling functions, so as to control or care for himself. For instance, he will be able at least a little to calm himself when upset, and not always need mother to pick him up and soothe him. These internalized concepts, the memories linked with emotions, help to sustain the relationship with mother when she is away, so the child can perhaps go to child care or be left with a sitter, without distress.

The child increasingly can communicate verbally, as well as with gestures about his experiences, questions, and ideas as his vocabulary increases. He can sometimes use words independently of actions: to talk *about* doing something rather than only doing it. He can talk about doing things that have not happened yet, as when he asks to be picked up, or to have a particular food. Because he has internal representations of these actions and objects well-established, he can think about the world in an "as-if" way.

By thirty-six months, generally the child has a large vocabulary intelligible to adults other than mother, with some phonetic substitutions. He talks to himself in long monologues, usually about the here-and-now including his pretend play, and he clearly has the ability to use his language to think about events, to imagine events that have not happened, and to plan for future events. He can generally refer to absent persons and events, calling up those memories and associated feelings by using the words learned with or about the absent persons or events.

The capacity to think about things that have not happened combines with the capacity to recognize that others see the world differently, and creates the beginnings of a capacity to lie: to present the world to the Other *as one wishes them to see it,* not as one believes it truly is. As we are learning that others think about us, we learn to care about *what* they think, and then we may begin to try to change what they think, by our behavior. Saying that what is inside our head—what we think/feel/remember—matches what is inside their head—what they desire—is a way to elicit a positive reaction. And since they know what is inside our head only as it is expressed in our behavior, including our words, it becomes possible to lie to others.

The child also is beginning to "lie" to himself, in pretend play, using symbols to express ideas, wishes, and fears and to manage those wishes and fears. His relationships with others are increasingly complicated and he clearly now has psychologically-driven ways of reacting to others. He may for instance be more comfortable with female strangers than with male strangers, even though neither has had any previous negative interaction. Child psychotherapists and psychoanalysts would consider it perhaps unusual, but not impossible, to involve a thirty month old verbal child in individual play therapy, because that child is able to use his internal models of the world to find ways to manage his emotional reactions to the world he lives in, and he can communicate through play with some words about his internal experience.

By around thirty-six months, we are no longer able to describe the "average predictable" developmental path, because the influences of family, environment, and the outside world are so powerful and disparate. Development—whether of language or of any other ego function or skill—is not a linear process. The child learns from his environment, but his responses to it also affect the environment, which then affects him again. It is not only the child who builds internal representations of mother. Mother also builds internal representations of her baby, and learns to see her relationship with him in ways that shape her reactions to him. A mother may describe her children as being "always strong-minded," or say that he "never really warmed up." In reaction she behaves with him *as if* he is stubborn or noncompliant or distant and unloving. If she sees him as "very friendly" she may feel always welcomed and loved, or perhaps she feels jealously that others are loved more than she is. All of these things affect how she behaves with him and the language she uses with him; and the way she behaves with him and the language she uses with him become a part of the emotional resonance of the words he is learning and using. The same is true for all other important people in the child's life. As Justin Call remarks (1980), we use language to create and maintain our social environment, our object relations. We use it both to communicate with others and to maintain our mental representations, when we use words to remember them; and the words we choose affect both the memory and the communication.

Children proceed through these stages at differing rates, influenced both by nature and nurture. Some families have a strong constitutional preference for action over words, and children in those families are slower to turn to language. Other families are more comfortable with "long distance," primarily verbal relationships than they are with close physical contact, so language comes earlier. In both sorts of families, some children "match" the family temperament while other children do not. Family style and family-infant match affect the rate and course of language acquisition by weakening or intensifying the emotional reward for communicating.

Language development is closely tied to the mother-child relationship. If mother is lost, or becomes unable to respond because of depression or other issues, the child may experience some regression or delay in language. Other sorts of stress, of course, may also lead to regression, although we know from many studies (Anna Freud, 1973) that mother's calm supportive presence provides some protection from stress-induced regression. Current work in parenting clearly suggests that helping mothers to maintain their own emotional equilibrium, and to put words to their children's feelings for themselves and for the child, helps the children to manage their feelings and to learn appropriate behavior (Etezady and Davis, 2012).

In later stages of language development we increasingly are able to substitute words for action, using "trial action" as we think or talk about what we want to do. When the baby says "No, no" and stops his action, he is substituting words for action. Parents and teachers often will tell young children to "use your words" in trying to help them learn to behave appropriately with other children and with family.

Language becomes progressively more grammatically complex as we grow and we use it for growing reality testing as well as more sophisticated thinking. Anny Katan (1961) looked at some of the ways spoken language contributes to the development of psychic structure, the way we organize our thinking and our ways of dealing with others and with the world. She demonstrated that being able to verbalize our perceptions of the outer world is a necessary precursor for verbalization of our feelings. Being able to verbalize feelings, impulses, and wishes, in turn, increases our ability to control affects and drives as well as our ability to distinguish between wishes or fantasies and reality. This ability then enhances the development of reality testing and secondary process, or conscious and logical, thought. Similarly, in 1966 Peller remarked "the acquisition of language activates the child's latent ability to bestow conceptual order on his experience" (p. 460): i.e., language makes possible a coherent understanding of the self and the world.

But semantic meaning and cognitive structure are not all there is to language. Language also conveys emotion, and assists us in learning to regulate our emotions (Katan, 1961). There is a general understanding throughout the literature (Katan, 1961; Call, 1980; Ogden, 1997; Pally, 2001) that the ability to talk about one's internal experience is crucial to the ability to manage one's emotions without acting out.

In our early years, our relationship with mother is how we manage our internal tension. Mother holds us and comforts us with words as well as touch, and the words become tied in our memory to the experience of being comforted. As we grow and internalize this experience, we learn to use words to comfort ourselves. When we are able to do this, it is because the emotional resonances of our words recall that early experience. Since that early relationship is different for each mother-child dyad, the emotional resonance of the words will be different for each of us.

In intimate relationships, sometimes we use our words to try to comfort others as our mother comforted us, or to deal with those others about the relationship. But because the emotional resonance of the words is different for speaker than for listener, what we convey is not always what we intend; and when others deal with us in feeling-full ways, what we hear is not always what is meant by the speaker. As Barth (1998) tells us, we take it for granted that we are speaking the same language as the other, but that may not always be true. "Mother" for one person, for instance, may be gentle, soft, and permissive; and for another be critical and demanding. In intimate relationships, we can sometimes avoid conflict or misunderstanding if we remember the words of the person we are speaking with have a different history than our own words. In psychotherapy and psychoanalysis, remembering this is an essential element to the work. We look for the ways our patient's history, as reflected in his use of his words, shapes his relationships. We discover his history most often through the transference, as he responds with feeling to our words and to his own. As we uncover that historical information, we understand how our patient's lives have shaped their relationships to words and how those lives and the accompanying words in turn shape their relationships to others.

By about thirty-six months, most children have nearly completed their acquisition of their primary language. They will continue to develop vocabulary and their relationship to grammar and syntax will become more complex and sophisticated. But by the time they are ready to begin preschool or kindergarten (in America), generally, their use of language is the lovely and sophisticated tool we all use, then, for the balance of our lives.

Some children, however, have encountered blocks to normal development, either because of life events or because of biological (constitutional or acquired) impediments to acquiring language. When the language acquisition process is derailed, necessarily the internal psychological capacities that accompany that development are also derailed, and so the child's ability to function in the world will be distorted. In the next chapter, we examine a few of the ways normal development may go astray.

Chapter Six

Interferences with Normal Development

We have seen how the mother-child interaction in the early months of life lays the groundwork for language, for emotional meanings of words, and for most of the capacities for verbal communication and emotion regulation in adult life. But what happens when that groundwork is faulty? When mother is deaf, and cannot speak to her child, how does the child learn that he can call mother from another room? When the child is deaf, how does he learn that vocal noises have communicative meaning, or find other ways to communicate with his environment? Deafness is the most obvious of the biological issues that can interfere with language acquisition. But other things may also impede this process. Blindness can interfere with the mix of verbal and nonverbal communication between mother and child, placing more emphasis on sound and voice than on the total experience; mental illness in the primary caretaker may interfere with her ability to enter into the full relationship of the mother-child dyad; autistic spectrum disorders can interfere with the child's innate ability to acquire the sorts of social meaning to words that we tend to take for granted. There are as yet no grand "unified field" theories of language acquisition that can provide answers to these questions. Chomsky's concept (1965) of a language acquisition device (LAD), a hypothesized instinctive mental capacity that enables an infant to acquire and produce language, comes closest. On examination, however, the LAD appears to be simply a metaphor for processes that are poorly understood, concretized to a sort of "black box" where the child's experiences go into the box and come out as language.

THE PRELINGUAL DEAF CHILD

There is ample evidence that for the deaf child language acquisition depends primarily on early communication with caretakers (Brinich, 1981; Wallis, Musselman, and Mackay, 2004; Freedman and Hansen, 1985). For the deaf child with deaf parents, communicating with American Sign Language (ASL) or some other type of Sign from early on, the pattern of development closely approximates that seen in hearing children of hearing parents. The hearing parents of some deaf children recognize the deafness early, and learn to Sign so that they may communicate with their child. These children also appear to have close to normal patterns of language acquisition, although there may be some lag and temporal delay in that essentially normal pattern. Children whose parents do not Sign, and who do not themselves learn to use Sign until later, such as when they enter school, do least well in acquiring language and, in adolescence, in measures of overall mental health (Wallis, Musselman, and MacKay, 2004).

This pattern of findings about language acquisition suggests clearly that it is the capacity to communicate within a meaningful caretaking relationship that allows for the development of language (either spoken language or Sign, which has all the characteristics of a true language) and of the related intrapsychic capacities. Although the question is not directly addressed in research that I reviewed, as best I can tell language acquisition with sign language is as satisfactory for later emotional and psychological development as is language acquisition with English, Japanese, or any vocal language. Because fully developed sign languages do have the characteristics of a true language, and are as useful for emotion-filled communication, we would not expect a difference developmentally when Sign is the native language.

HEARING CHILDREN OF DEAF PARENTS

Hearing children of deaf parents pose a different problem. For these children, the relationship with mother is interrupted not because they cannot take in mother's verbal stimuli, but because mother does not respond to the child's vocal stimuli, interrupting the early "attunement" that is so important. Most of the literature which I found on this topic dealt only with language acquisition itself, without considering the effects of that process on emotional and psychological development. In a review of research on these issues, Schiff-Meyers (1993) reports that for the most part, hearing children of deaf parents are able to develop normal speech and language if the family life is otherwise normal and if they have exposure to normal hearing speakers (5–10 hours a week, not only on television). There may at times be early problems with enunciation and syntax, and the children's early utterances sometimes mimic the syntactic structure of the sign language used by the parents. Again, however, the critical factor appears to be the relational interaction and communication, the opportunity to learn that some symbols—either sounds or gestures—have meaning, that the meaning conveyed can be used to affect one's environment, and that the meaning can reflect one's internal experience. For children who are already using Sign, learning a spoken language appears to play the same role, neither more nor less significant, as learning a second spoken language plays for normally hearing children.

BLIND CHILDREN

It is not intuitively obvious that blind children would have difficulties in language acquisition, but as we consider the early interaction of mother and child questions begin to come up. At the age when the baby recognizes mother's face, how does he recognize mother when he cannot see her? How does he know that she is anywhere in the room? How does mother initiate the sort of pre-lingual play that for a hearing child begins with making faces? How does the baby learn to recognize the nonverbal elements of language, such as facial expression and cues for turn-taking? Since the infant's capacity to follow an adult's gaze predicts later language competence (Meltzoff and Brooks, 2009), what happens when the infant *cannot* follow the adult gaze, because he cannot perceive it?

Of course the mutual focus of attention of mother and child is affected when a child is blind: mother cannot follow her child's curious gaze and comment on what she sees because there is no gaze to follow. The baby cannot gaze into mother's face as he is fed, and they will not smile at each other. Gestures of both baby and parent will be useless, because the baby is unlikely to make any gestures toward objects that he cannot see, and he cannot see the gestures that mother makes. The blind baby's dwelling in the world must be mediated by senses other than vision, such as touch, voice, and smell. If mother keeps the child near her, talks to him almost constantly and plays with him, providing nonverbal evidence of her existence, he can develop a solid sense of her presence and they will create a mutually pleasurable bond (Wills, 1979), much as sighted children do. Without that constant non-visual input, however, the baby's ability to connect solidly to mother is lost.

The attunement of mother and child, the ability for each to recognize the mood of the other and to adapt to the other, will also be impaired for the blind baby. He cannot recognize the early signs of mother's displeasure (her frown) when he cries for no reason, and so he has less motivation to substitute controlled vocalization for his crying. Mother in turn cannot catch the baby's eye and share his pleasure in a new experience. She will not see that the baby is intrigued by a toy, or a color, or an object, and then name it for him; she cannot engage his visual attention in something that she finds intriguing. In her review of the literature, Anne Mills (1993) finds that failure of the parent to notice nonvisual signals indicating attention and concentration is associated with the child's failure to develop normal communication and language.

Visually impaired children do follow a generally normal path of vocabulary acquisition, but it tends to be somewhat delayed (Mills, 1993; Fraiberg, 1968). In addition, Dorothy Wills (1979) remarks that the blind child's language is "not *closely* linked with meaning" (p. 85). She goes on to remind us that "sight is the great organizer of perception: without it many sense impressions...are sequential and not easily organized into a whole" (p. 90). Some events heard at a distance cannot be understood merely by listening. The blind child thus requires more time to understand his world, and needs more support from his mother to find the context for his fragmented experiences. He may need physical contact in order to integrate and make sense of his disparate perceptions. To understand this problem, one need only remember the story of the blind men and the elephant: each could understand only the part of the whole animal that he could feel and touch, and none could put the parts together into a whole. Where sighted children can explore the world with their gaze, learning new things as they move through it, blind children can fully explore only the part of the world within their touch. Hearing allows them to know that something is happening, but likely not at first to make full sense of it; and they may not recognize that static, nonmoving objects exist at all. It will take them longer to locate themselves within the wider world of senses and distant objects. Likely it also takes them longer to recognize and understand inanimate portions of their environment, and perhaps interferes with vocabulary acquisition for non-animate nouns or even for verbs. How does one distinguish a chair from a table, or dropping something from hitting something, without seeing it?

Fraiberg and Adelson (1973) tell us that in children blind from birth there is often a delay in the stable acquisition of the pronoun "I," reflecting most likely a delay in development of a solid self-representation. The "I" that reflects need or want in "Iwanna" arrives at the expected time, and many language achievements fall within the range anticipated for sighted children. However, there is a delay in the capacity to disengage the "I" of "Iwanna" for use in new combinations such as "I see" or "I walk." The flexible and changing use of "I" reflects the child's capacity to represent himself "as an 'I' in a universe of 'I's" (Fraiberg and Adelson, 1973, p. 540). This lag in development, which extends to other self-referential pronouns, has generally disappeared by age six, when the children begin school. Fraiberg and Adelson see it as reflecting the reality that developing self-representation for the blind child must occur without "the single sensory organ that is uniquely adapted for synthesis of all perceptions and the data of self" (p. 558). The blind child is unable to perceive an entire large object in a single perceptual action—seeing—but must do so sequentially, by touching all parts of it and integrating the sensations in his mind. In the same way, he is unable to perceive himself in one perceptual event, but must find ways to recognize himself in the context of the world to which he is blind. It thus will require more capacity to synthesize and integrate perceptions to be able to make sense of those perceptions, which not surprisingly occurs later than for sighted children. This delay in understanding the world around him must necessarily be reflected in a delay in how he talks about the world around him, and how he uses language to find himself in that world.

FERAL CHILDREN

As we consider acquisition of language that occurs in "exceptional circumstances"—circumstances other than normal development—we inevitably encounter instances of children who presumably had a reasonably normal endowment, but whose early years were so deprived of normal interaction that when discovered they were considered "feral," almost not human because of the impoverishment of their early years. Few of these cases have been closely studied, one hopes because there are few to study. There are, however, several which are discussed repeatedly in the available literature.

Genie (Curtiss, 1977; Skuse, 1993) spent her life from twenty months to thirteen years seven months confined to a small room, usually strapped into an infant's potty chair or confined in a strait-jacket-like "sleeping bag," and fed only infant food. She was tended by her visually impaired mother, who escaped with her when Genie was thirteen. After the escape, Genie was cared for by a foster family, and showed some improvement but "never acquired true linguistic competence" (Skuse, 1993).

Mary and Louise (Skuse, 1984, 1993) were sisters who had been kept tied on leashes to a bed until aged three years six months (Louise) and two years four months (Mary) by their microcephalic, mentally retarded, and mentally ill mother. When removed from the home, they "took no notice of anything or anyone except to scamper up and sniff strangers, grunting and snuffling like animals." After being placed in a small children's home, run as a family unit, both made initial rapid gains in both verbal and nonverbal abilities. Louise went on to achieve normal language competence. Mary, who was also microcephalic, displayed a number of autistic behaviors and never achieved normal language. It seems likely that her failure to develop normal language relates to her biologically faulty endowment (due to microcephaly) rather than to environmental issues.

Anna (Davis, 1947; Skuse, 1993; Freedman, 1981) was found at age five tied to a chair in an old storage room in her farm home. She had apparently been there since infancy, with her arms tied above her head. She was unable to talk or move and was extraordinarily frail, most likely due to never having received adequate nourishment. On removal from the home she was initially placed in a county home for the aged and infirm, where one nurse cared for 300 inmates, but was transferred to a foster home nine months later. In the foster home she showed rapid improvement in motor and cognitive skills. After nine months in the foster home she was placed in a private home for retarded children, where she made few further advances, although she did begin to develop speech after two years in this placement. At her death three years after the final placement, she was reported to be repeating single words and to be able to attempt conversation.

Isabelle (Mason, 1942; Skuse, 1993; Freedman, 1981) was discovered at six-and-a-half, having spent her life in seclusion with her deaf-mute mother in a dark room away from all contact. When mother escaped with her, her behavior was "that of a 'wild animal'" (Skuse, 1993, making "a strange croaking sound" in lieu of speech. Once in hospital for physiotherapy and surgery (for rickets and physical problems related to the early deprivation), she quickly began to attempt vocalization, passing through normal developmental stages at a greatly accelerated pace. Within a year she was able to read and write with "fair competence," and after only eighteen months she had a vocabulary of 2000 words and was able to use imaginative play.

The conclusion which I draw from these cases is that interpersonal interaction is a primary key to language development. In all cases where there was a positive individual relationship with a nurturing caretaker, eventual language development was significantly more complete. For Isabelle, who had such a relationship with her deaf-mute mother, her acquisition of language was remarkable, with vocalization beginning only one week after her rescue. This suggests to me that the relational aspect of language—the idea that meaning can be carried between people—had been established, and it lacked only the opportunity to learn to vocalize for her to be able to use the relational principle to develop oral speech. Although I have only second hand (and in some cases third hand) reports, it is my impression that the children who had the most complete formation of language were those who had at least some early interaction with a loving caretaker, and those who had more individual attention (in family settings rather than large institutions) after rescue from the deprivation.

LANGUAGE ACQUISITION WITH PERCEPTUAL DISABILITY

The development of language almost by definition requires the capacity to recognize an "other" in the world outside oneself. A central motivation for language acquisition is to connect with the other, and to find ways to keep the other "with" us as we learn that we are single individuals, isolated in the privacy of our own minds. Sensory perception is how we find the other in the world, and so any compromise of that sensory perception must interfere at least slightly with the capacity and motivation to connect. David Freedman (1981) suggests that our perception of the object—of mother—is the product of a synthesis of visual perception, auditory perception, and somesthetic perception (touch, smell, taste). He believes that any one of these modalities of perception can be absent without interfering with the child's ability to develop the internal representations that allow for normal psychic structure. The internal representation of mother, in turn, allows us to know that there is an "other" to reach out to, and so provides the motivation and energy to reach out to her through language.

INDIVIDUALS ON THE AUTISTIC SPECTRUM

So now we come to the individual who has all the physical and cognitive abilities to use language fully, and who has had the early caretaking which is so critical, but who nevertheless seems in some way not to be able to make use of the emotional aspect of words. Individuals on the autistic spectrum appear to have this sort of linguistic dysfunction as a central issue.

The autistic spectrum ranges from true autism on one end of the spectrum, with profoundly impaired individuals who may have little or no speech and very poor cognitive functioning, to individuals with Asperger's syndrome on the other end. Asperger's syndrome is characterized primarily by difficulties in social interaction, along with restricted and repetitive patterns of interest and behavior. Intelligence is usually normal or even above average, and linguistic competence appears intact, with difficulties in social interaction that arise from inability to understand the emotional aspects of relationships and of words. Between Asperger's syndrome and severe autism lies the wide range of individuals with pervasive developmental disorder: delays or distortions of development in all significant areas of functioning, more severe than Asperger's syndrome but not so severe as to be labeled truly autistic.

Temple Grandin, a high-functioning autistic who would most likely today be described as suffering from Asperger's syndrome, has described in fascinating detail the way in which she "thinks in pictures" (1995, p. 11–22). Although she would be considered to have intact language, and in fact she writes eloquently and compellingly, words have a different utility for her than for many others. For Ms. Grandin, the power of language resides almost entirely in its capacity to represent concrete images. She says quite clearly that "autistics have problems learning things that cannot be thought about in pictures." For some, even written words are too abstract, and they learn to spell more easily using plastic letters that they can touch and feel (p. 13–14).

In her childhood and adolescence, Ms. Grandin says, she learned to convert abstract ideas into pictures as a way to understand them. In high school and college, she understood the concept of "getting on with the next step in [her] life" by finding a door that she could literally walk through. She prepared for college graduation by practicing physically walking through this door many times (p. 18), and the act of going through that door appears to have helped her to manage the anxiety about her uncertain future.

Other autistic individuals may not attend fully to spoken language. Theresa Joliffe (quoted in Grandin, 1995, pp. 67–68) has reported that she usually loses the first few words when spoken to because it takes her that long to recognize the communicative intent of the sounds. In her childhood, speech was no more meaningful to her than other sounds. It was only after seeing words written on paper that she was able to recognize them when spoken. Some nonverbal children can be taught to sing before they can speak, as the pairing of the words with the rhythm and melody seems to help the sound register as communication in some way (Grandin, 1995, p. 68).

The exact cause of autistic spectrum disorders is still unclear, although it is generally acknowledged that there is some biological underpinning. Research does indicate that there are associated brain abnormalities, with structural and functional differences in specific regions of the brain. The best we can do at this point for treatment interventions is to try to address the functional differences, including specifically speech and language dysfunction as this is reflected in social interactions.

INDIVIDUALS WITH ALEXITHYMIA

In 1967, Peter Sifneos identified a group of patients with psychosomatic disorders who had great difficulty in finding words to describe feelings, and coined the term "alexithymia" (literally, "no words for feelings") to describe them. Since that time, the concept of alexithymia has lurked on the fringes of psychiatry, psychology, and psychotherapy, never quite making it into the full light of day as an identifiable disorder. All therapists have seen at least a few patients who have marked difficulty in identifying, describing, and working with one's own feelings and who have difficulty recognizing the feelings of others. Often these people confuse their emotions with the bodily sensations that accompany the emotions. They tend to have a somewhat constricted capacity to imagine or to fantasize, with few dreams, and their thought patterns tend to be concrete, reality-based, and logical to the point of excluding emotional responses to events in their lives. Although they may mention anxiety or depression, they seem to have only poorly differentiated emotions, limiting their ability to discuss them with others.

Various psychoanalytic authors have addressed these issues, only a few of whom I have referenced here (Bollas 1987, Bromberg 1994, Gedo 1996, Krystal 1988, Stolorow and Atwood 1992). Several of them suggest, as does Diane Barth (1998), that addictions and other impulsive acting-out behaviors can be understood as attempts to process one's unarticulated overwhelming feelings when words are not useful for that purpose. Barth describes patients "who turn out to have surprising and subtle deficits in their ability to use words to symbolically communicate, represent, and process their emotions. . . . Living in a world in which there is a gap between the feelings they name and the frequently inchoate affects they experience, they can go through long and partially useful analyses without making significant changes in some of their most painful symptoms" (p. 686). For these people, language is not useful to capture their experience, although the words clearly have meaning to them. They are often able to "sound as though they know exactly what they are feeling and therefore seem capable of processing these experiences verbally" (Barth, 1998, p. 690). For these patients, however, as for Kay in chapter 1, words are not useful in that particular way.

Individuals who are unable to use words to express or describe their feelings will often use words very concretely, with no capacity to imagine a "what if" or to imagine that others might find ways to describe things that are different but also accurate: "Exploration of feeling becomes concretization of that feeling" (Barth, 1998, p. 692). They may, on the other hand, experience words as somehow fraudulent and unreal. They are both unable to genuinely or accurately communicate their feelings to someone else, and unable to fully experience those feelings themselves, as if it is only in the sharing of the feeling that it becomes real. I am reminded here of the way in which Kay was able, after several months of talking about the feelings associated with her paintings, to tell me that the images were not "really" true about her, much as we both hoped that they might be. It was only when we were able to go back and find what was "true," what was *hers* and not *mine*, that she began to be able to find images and visual metaphors of her own, with work in three dimensions and the story she told of going to sea, being first shipwrecked and then rescued.

There is much that we don't know about how these individuals function in daily life and in their inner experience. We can only speculate about what might have led to such an elusive and difficult-to-recognize distortion of the use of language. I believe that some subtle disruption of the early mother/ child dyad led to the acquisition of language useful more for hiding from the other than for revealing oneself. For these individuals, their language allows them to hide their true selves so successfully that even when they want to find themselves in their own words they cannot.

Hans Loewald noted, "The emotional relationship to the person from whom the word is learned plays a significant, in fact crucial, part in how alive the link between thing and word turns out to be" (1980, p. 197). For Kay, I suspect that there was a misattunement, a mismatch in mother's ability to recognize Kay's emotions and help her with them. Kay and her mother illustrate Rizzuto's 2003 assertion that "[a] child who learns to speak, but whose mother's language has not mirrored his/her inner experience, uses language in a way that does not engage the self" (p. 290). Because Kay's language did not *engage* her experience of self, she was unable to use the language to *mirror* her own inner experience at the beginning of the treatment.

One clue that Kay's mother was not able to recognize Kay's emotions clearly is the time in early adolescence when Kay's parents sought help for her because she was crying daily, only to cancel the appointment on the day it was due because she did not cry. I can only understand this failure to obtain help for a distressed child if I assume that mother took the not-crying as evidence that the distress was relieved, and so no help was needed. To me, at this time, that appears an obvious mistake; but mother's inability to look past surface behaviors to emotional reality is certainly reflected in Kay's original inability to look past the surface content of her paintings to the emotional reality which they expressed.

In our speculations about how alexithymic individuals developed their "surprising and subtle deficit," we begin with an assumption that at some point in their early life it served a useful function: that at some point it was necessary for them to hide emotions both from themselves and from others. Early in life we are reliant on our relationship with mother to manage our emotional lives: when we cry she picks us up and soothes us, or plays with us until we laugh with her. As we grow and learn to relate to the world, learning how to have an impact on the world and how to interact with others, we also learn that mother and others respond to events in the world with emotions. Some things make mother happy and some things upset her; most important-ly, perhaps, we learn that *we* can make mother happy, or can upset her, by our behaviors. Most children will at least initially try to avoid making mother unhappy, or will try to cheer her up. Georgina sometimes brings her young child, now two, to her psychotherapy sessions because she has no sitter. When Georgina cries or is distressed, the child will often look at her worried-ly, and may offer a toy, or may lean on her leg in an effort to comfort her.

In a family where the primary caretaker has problems managing her own emotions, not infrequently the child becomes a "regulator," and begins to feel responsible for the feelings of others. If mother cries every time the child is distressed, then the child must learn not to be distressed. If mother tells her son that "big boys don't cry," then the boy is likely to try very hard not to look as if he wants to cry, because he so much wants to be a "big boy" for mother.

We learn to control and contain our emotions in order to protect those around us, so that mother can be calm enough to care for us, in order to keep others happy, and so that we don't have to deal with the anger or fear or sadness of others when it is in response to our own anger or fear or sadness. As we learn to hide our feelings, we begin to learn to hide them even from ourselves, in order to protect ourselves from the uncomfortable feelings that accompany the frustrations of everyday life. As Winnicott (1960) says, "It seems necessary to allow for the concept of the isolation of [the] central self as a characteristic of health. Any threat to this isolation of the true self constitutes a major anxiety at this early stage, and defences of earliest infancy appear in relation to failures on the part of the mother (or in maternal care) to ward off impingements which might disturb this isolation" (p. 590).

As psychological development continues, and we make ourselves into who we will be as adults, the things that we have done within the early mother-child dyad to maintain our equilibrium often become things that we do within ourselves to maintain an emotional equilibrium: if we tried very hard not to look sad so as not to upset mother, we may try very hard not to look sad at all times, so as to protect ourselves from being upset. If mother was unable to tolerate emotional stress, we usually have problems as adults tolerating and containing the stresses of daily life. Our defenses—the patterns of behavior that help us to maintain our emotional equilibrium in the face of life stresses—almost always mirror our childhood experiences in some way.

I often see young women who to all appearances are cheerful, happy, and popular—but who tried to kill themselves. When they enter into treatment after a suicide threat or gesture, not infrequently what I hear is how empty they feel, how they do not know how to let others in to get to know them. They have worked so hard to protect themselves from the unhappinesses of daily life that they have emotionally disappeared. The "isolation of the true self" which Winnicott (1960, p. 590) saw as necessary has grown and taken over until these girls have isolated their *entire* selves, not only the fragile frightened part of themselves. They have never learned to manage how to reveal parts of themselves and conceal other parts by what they choose to say and how they choose to say it; rather they have concealed the entirety of their self, and the reciprocal interactions with others that feed us and sustain us are missing from their emotional experiences. To establish the interpersonal connections that allow one to be not-alone in the world, language must be emotionally meaningful and useful for conveying the essence of oneself to others, useful for revealing and not only for hiding.

Chapter Seven

The Language of Trauma

Speaking the Unspeakable

As we have seen, our histories are reflected in our language. From the most obvious effect, the particular dialect of the particular language we speak, to more subtle effects, such as the words we use for family members ("Mom" or "Mother," "Daddy" or "Father"), information about our lives and our history is embedded in the words we speak. The words we speak then, in turn, affect our present and our future, as we use language to bring others closer or to push them away, to show ourselves to others or to hide ourselves, to find our place in the world of relationships.

Of all clinical situations where the subtleties of language affect our daily lives and reveal our histories, work with individuals whose past includes significant trauma[1] illustrates the issue perhaps most clearly. From the ways that these people live their lives, to the ways that they relate to others, to the ways that we deal with them in psychotherapeutic work, we see the effects of trauma. We see the effects of trauma also in the language which traumatized individuals use to talk about themselves, and in the language which we must use in order to help them heal.

Trauma by definition refers to events that are "shattering, devastating, causing internal disruption by putting ego functioning and ego mediation out of action" (A. Freud, 1969, p. 238): our reactions to traumatic events interfere with the ability of our conscious minds to deal effectively with external reality. Speaking about our experiences is one of the ways that we deal with external reality, as we express our emotional reactions and as we ask others for help in managing. But as Constance Dalenberg (2000, p. 57) says, "Trau-

ma is hard to speak and hard to hear." There are no words that are adequate
to capture either the experience of a true trauma, or the emotional response
when one hears about it. Most often the victim of severe trauma is at first
unable to speak clearly about his experience, and very often he is unable to
engage others to help him manage his reactions to the experience. It is my
impression that this inability to speak or to ask for help is particularly true for
individuals who have survived traumatic experiences at the hands of other
people, as in war, abuse, or torture, more than for individuals who are the
survivors of natural disasters such as tornados or hurricanes. Perhaps the
knowledge that the harm occurred within a relationship, at the hands of
others, interferes with being able to use different relationships to undo the
harm. The people whom I describe here have suffered immense damage at
the hands of others, and I can only marvel at the courage it takes to reveal
oneself to yet another person who may hurt you yet again.

The individual who was traumatized is often unable to speak of his experience in part because of shame ("it's my fault, I shouldn't have been so
needy"), guilt ("it's my fault, I made my father mad"), for fear of being hurt
again ("if I tell anyone, he'll find out and kill me" even though the abuser is
dead), or for many other essentially illogical reasons. Once he overcomes the
illogic, and begins to try to talk about what was done to him, he may also be
unable to speak of the experience because the activation of traumatic memory reduces the perfusion of Broca's area, the part of the brain that mediates
expressive speech (Rauch et al., 1996). Reducing the blood supply to Broca's
area inhibits its function, and sometimes these individuals are literally unable
to find the words to speak.

Janet, who has a horrific history of abuse as a child, will begin to stammer
when things arise that stir her memories or her fears of being hurt or abandoned. She has at times spent close to ten minutes struggling to finish even
one word, trying desperately to talk to me because she knows I want to help,
because she wants to please me, because she must speak her terror; but she is
unable to do so. At these times, my impulse is always to tell her that she need
not speak, that she need not struggle so terribly to do the impossible, but I
know that even though she cannot speak of her internal terrors, she must, in
order ever to be free of the terror and in order to be able to speak freely of
other things. When we are unable to speak of events in the past, we are
vulnerable to reliving them in the present: "Whatever is unresolved and
unsayable repeats" (Rogers, 2006, p. 97). Much of the work that Janet and I
have done over the years has been simply finding ways to help her to speak
about her fear and about the unspeakable things that happened to her.

In working with Janet and others with similar histories of terrible trauma,
we sometimes find that we must approach difficult issues at a slant. We must
allow long silences, or a change of subject, without challenging it. Janet often
is not able to tell me what she is thinking in response to a question or a

comment from me. At these junctures in our work together, I sometimes feel as if I am walking a tightrope. If I simply wait, she may feel that I am "zoning out," that I am thinking about something else, that I am not engaged with her. If I ask her to say something, however, or push for a verbal response to my question or comment, she may feel that I am impatient and irritable, that she is failing to be a "good patient." Every communication between us requires that I make a deliberate conscious effort to determine how Janet is feeling on that particular day at that particular time, in order to think about how she might hear what I say and to decide how long to wait or not wait for her to speak.

Once I have determined that I should speak and not wait longer, the question of what to say arises. Janet already has said that she cannot tell me what she is thinking about my remark. When she is able to tell me her next thought, even if it seems irrelevant, that thought may provide clues. In one such exchange, we were talking about her sense of being disconnected from me. I had learned that this is usually a clue that Janet was seeing me as being in some way like all the adults who had not protected her from her various abusers: feeling that I was not listening to her, that I was indifferent, or that I was being critical of her. When I asked if she had an idea about what had strained our relationship, she did not. But when I asked what (perhaps unrelated) thoughts were going through her head, she told me several anecdotes about her day where people in her office had failed to meet their job expectations, or had been late for appointments, or had not provided what she needed to do her own job. As I listened, I heard the pattern of relationship failure, of people not doing what was expected and needed, and I began to think about what I might have done to fail Janet in some way. In my long history with Janet, I had found that most of the time the seemingly unrelated thoughts that arose at times like this in fact were versions in the "outside world" of what she felt was happening in our "inside world." I had learned that patterns heard in her account of her day might be directly related to patterns between us; and so I had learned that asking about her seemingly unrelated thoughts was a way to help her let me know what was happening between us. She could not speak about us, but her unconscious could filter the events of her life and find things that were both sayable and, in some more-or-less distant and manageable way, similar.

In this particular exchange, I also thought about Janet's common fear that she had failed me, that she was disappointing me and not doing what I wanted from her. I chose on this day *not* to wait for her to speak, because she seemed more than usually vulnerable to shame and fear of failure. Then I remembered that in a previous session I had forgotten something Janet had told me. Her comment in the previous session had been important to her in ways that were not clear to me, and it fell out of my memory. I reminded Janet at this time of my lapse of memory, and said that I suspected that she was feeling that I—like the people at work, and ultimately like her mother—had ignored her needs. I went on to say that I believed that she was not able to tell me this because she feared I would feel criticized, and would then be enraged and either kill her or abandon her (a recurring fear which she had previously come to recognize). On one level she knew that I would do neither; but on the emotional level, where our unconscious reactions live, she absolutely feared that I would be like her abuser or her neglectful and abusive mother, and so she felt at risk. She was not able to speak up to avoid that risk by reminding me of my omission, however, because she feared that criticizing me would *turn me into* someone like the abuser or the neglectful mother, and so she would again be at risk.

For the victims of severe trauma, much of their life is this sort of dilemma: they feel frightened and at risk, but the behaviors necessary to avoid the risk are themselves dangerous and risky, and so they cannot save themselves. They are caught in a perpetual state of fear and panic, feeling as if the trauma is about to recur, and there is nothing they can do to avoid it. Because usually they know with their conscious minds that this is not true, they are at a loss to explain to themselves the reason for their chronic fear, and so they feel stupid, or cowardly, or find some other way of explaining themselves to themselves, an explanation that perpetuates their emotional pain. They are unable to speak clearly about either the dilemma or about how they try to manage it.

One of our first tasks in working with these individuals is to find a way to reduce and soften the chronic shame and guilt they live with, so that they can talk with us about it, and can make use of treatment. They are ashamed of what happened to them, often blaming themselves; they are ashamed of how hard it is for them to talk about it; they are ashamed sometimes that they exist at all. To be able to work with them and not drive them away in their shame, we must pay close attention to using language that is not shaming. We must struggle to remember that even when we are not *feeling* accusatory or blaming, what we say may be heard that way. In my own practice, I try to remark on emotions experienced more than on behaviors: for instance, "It's so hard when you want your mother to notice what you did, but you think she'll just tell you it's no good. Sometimes all you know how to do is to break something, so she'll at least know you're there!" I am always careful not to use words suggesting that what they have done is "wrong" or "bad" lest I turn into the critical mother; rather I try to frame our discussion in terms of what works for them and what does not work for them.

I also find it necessary at times to talk with my patients about what is average expectable behavior: for instance, when someone says something mean to you, it is not surprising that you get angry. If Janet ever got angry, however, she was beaten, and she learned very early on that getting angry is dangerous. Individuals with histories of chronic abuse within their families may have little or no sense of what sorts of responses to life events are reasonable and what sorts of responses are dysfunctional. Helping them to recognize how others react to life events, and to acknowledge that the "rules" of life are not different for them than for others, can help to give them permission to advocate for themselves, or to defend themselves when others try to take advantage of them. Talking about these issues gives our patients words to use within themselves at crisis points, much as a small child may repeat mother's words of reassurance when doing something difficult.

Many therapists who work with traumatized patients find that they do a certain amount of "mentoring," of helping the patient to think about ways of behaving in the wider community that will work to achieve their goals and to understand which will perpetuate their problem situations. We talk about the feelings that come up in daily frustrations and life problems, recognizing that everyone has similar feelings. Putting those feelings into words and "normalizing" them makes use of the potential for words to contain emotions, helping to build the patient's ability to manage his own emotions even in difficult situations.

In working with traumatized individuals, we also find that our own emotions about what we are hearing may interfere with being fully present. In my own writing about these individuals, I find (as in this chapter) that I often use language that is somewhat more distant, more intellectualized, and less experience-near than the language I use for discussing less damaged persons. In working with our patients, we must take care not to take an emotional step back, to remove ourselves from the experience which we are sharing. If we allow our own grief, rage, and anxiety about what our patients underwent to distance us from the emotions, we risk abandoning them to their own grief, rage, and terror. This may serve to convince them that we believe they deserved the victimization, and becomes yet another victimization for them.

As we work with our patients to learn how to be in the world without perpetuating dysfunctional patterns of behavior—patterns learned in dysfunctional families—we are reminded that what is unresolved and unsayable will repeat. We find that trauma victims do repeat their trauma in everyday life, in obvious as well as more subtle ways.

In *The Unsayable: The Hidden Language of Trauma,* Annie Rogers (2006) provides a poignant description of some of the ways that trauma victims are constrained to express their trauma in everyday language without forcing recognition into their conscious minds. She describes the Lacanian idea that we all have "two levels of speaking, one that we know what we are saying…and another that we have no idea of what we are saying. In this second level of speaking there are repeating words, phrases, and even sounds that function as magnets of unconscious meaning. . . ." (p. 80). She goes on to talk about a girl (pp. 95–209) who had been molested by a babysitter named Ed, and who talked about her head (=Ed?) hurting, of headaches (Ed aches). In various ways, with multiple different syllables, words, and sounds, the trauma was recalled in ways that the girl herself did not recognize until it was highlighted by Dr. Rogers. Recognizing these "echoes" of the trauma was central to the work of the therapy and to allowing the girl to find new ways of reacting to her life experiences.

In psychotherapeutic work with traumatized individuals, it is more common than not to find that our patients cannot talk openly about their histories or about their feelings. Like Janet, when the traumatic memories are activated, Broca's area shuts down and they are simply unable to find words. Even when Janet can do more than stammer, she is usually unable to talk about herself or about the memories or feelings: the best she can do is to tell me stories of her day that may give me a clue about what themes are hidden in her silence. Silence itself can be both healing and overwhelming. For Janet, on some days it is important that I am able to wait and listen as she struggles to talk, or sit with her as she is sad and fearful, sharing the experience with her. On other days it is important that I be more active in helping her to find her way into talking about the experience. On some days she feels that saying anything about her grief, rage, and fear is "only whining," and so she tries to be strong and silent. On other days she knows that talking about her feelings helps her to contain them, that she can speak and I can hear and then she is not alone with them. The art of the work lies in finding the nonverbal and verbal cues that tell me what she needs on any given day.

Sometimes whether I speak or not has little to do with what my patient might need. Every therapist who works with severely traumatized individuals has had the experience of not knowing what to say when we truly comprehend the disaster which our patient experienced. How can I say to a survivor of the attack on the twin towers in New York that I understand how it felt to see "people falling out of the buildings like rain"? Dalenberg (2000) writes at length about the inadequacy of language to convey these experiences. She describes situations where the "fragmented, silence-ridden language of the trauma victim" led to the therapist perceiving the patient as resisting the therapy. At the same time, the therapist's silence in the face of horror—because there are no words to convey one's grief and rage at the knowledge of how the other was hurt—was experienced by the patient as an unwillingness to listen to the patient's struggles to speak. Dalenberg goes on to suggest that both patient and therapist must "give up the belief that perfect articulation is possible, and instead…struggle together to reach a good-enough disclosure"; that both must accept a "controlled inaccuracy" (p. 62) in descriptions of the traumatic experience and in conveying their own responses to the patient's history.

The patient often knows that he needs to find words for his experience but that he is unable. His "tension between the necessity to describe and the felt incapacity to do so" (Dalenberg, 2000, p. 66) resides alongside the therapist's tension between the need to understand and the fear that verbalizing understanding will be experienced as insincere or hypocritical, since the words of understanding are also inadequate to fully expressing or explaining the emotions. We know that our patients need us to hear and to understand, to feel their suffering with them at least partially and incompletely. And yet we have our own resistance, our own wish not to feel the emotional pain; and we want to convey our understanding without causing our patient even more pain; and sometimes we are unable to hear or to understand because it is simply too much. How do I tell Janet that I understand her terror as, at 4, she watched her mother murder her baby brother and then come to murder her? How *can* I understand that terror? There are very simply no words to convey what the experience was like for that child, what the memory is like for the adult, or what it is like for me to hear and to know about that nightmare, and to know what living through the nightmare has done to this woman. If I talk about it at all, I risk minimizing the intensity of the emotion and seeming to be emotionally disconnected, or I risk being overwhelmed by my own (as well as Janet's) grief, rage, and fear, and then I become unavailable as a support, not strong enough to be able to help her.

As we will see in chapter 8, we sometimes are able to find ways of talking about things that cannot be talked about. There are no words that can match the intensity of the feelings for these patients. The way we use language, however, can be transformed and transformative, and our language then becomes a powerful tool in helping our patients. In Dalenberg's book *Countertransference and the Treatment of Trauma* (2000), she presents an extended clinical vignette (pp. 63–65) where she and her patient together found a new meaning for a word that had been, in the mouth of the child's father, derogatory, but in Dr. Dalenberg's mouth became praise. The father had repeatedly told this child that she was just a "little bit of nothing" who could never do anything worthwhile; Dalenberg talked about how little bits of nothing in computers can, in the right place, do marvelous and powerful things. With Dr. Dalenberg, the patient was able to *choose* to hear the phrase "little bit of nothing" in a different way than she had originally, and to be proud of herself rather than ashamed. The ability of this therapeutic dyad to mobilize the multi-layered nature of language, turning to the positive meaning that can live alongside the negative, was powerful and transformative.

Sometimes we can "reframe," or find new meanings for words, in ways that allow us to shift our feelings at least slightly, as did Dalenberg's patient. We also use similes, metaphors, analogies, poetry, and many different ways of finding expression for the things we need to express, even as the girl described by Rogers in *The Unsayable* (2006) found ways to allow the memory of the abuse into her everyday speech, as syllables and sounds. Metaphors and similes in particular can be helpful tools, as they allow us to talk about difficult events with a "controlled inaccuracy" that comes close enough to reach some of the feelings but not so close that we are overwhelmed and incapacitated by the feelings. To say that Janet is "drowning" in her feelings and that I threw her a lifeline (or at times that I failed to do so, that I let her drown) conveys a part of our relatedness that we have not found other words for. Using the same metaphor, Janet has been able to tell me that "drowning in an inch of water is not any better than drowning in six feet of water": this captured for me clearly her feeling of being overwhelmed at the moment, even though I felt correctly that she had progressed significantly in being able to manage her emotions. She was able, at other times, to agree that she had progressed, but when she felt she was drowning, she was still drowning, even though the "surface" of the emotions, and survival, was not as hard to reach as it had been initially.

The double-edged sword of language allows us to talk about things for which there are no words. But in using metaphors and similes, if we forget that what we are expressing is only a figure of speech, we can fall into error. Individuals with severe histories of trauma again offer us a way to look at this issue clearly, in the form of a clinical disorder which has over the years aroused a great deal of controversy.

Dissociative identity disorder (DID), for which the old name is "multiple personality disorder," evolves in an individual as a defense against severe and usually chronic trauma: the child who is repeatedly abused horrifically, the adult who is tortured. The event is so terrible that the only way they have to survive is essentially to not be: to convince themselves that what is happening is not happening to them, but to someone else. For some, this takes the form of an out-of-body experience, where they can see what is happening but do not experience it as happening to their own body, and so do not have the physical pain or the emotional agony that accompanies it. For others, usually children who are repeatedly and chronically abused, they "create" another self, who becomes the self that experiences the abuse, protecting the "core self"—the original self—from the pain and terror, and from the memory of the experience. They do not experience themselves as having a continuous chronological life; rather they experience themselves as having gaps of time where they do not know what has happened. Later they are told that they have done things they do not remember doing, or they never know what has happened during the "lost" time. At other times, they experience themselves as being someone different, the person who did the things that the "core self" does not remember. At those times they do not remember ever "being" the core self. They have, as a psychological defense against their intolerable fear, anger, and grief, adopted a metaphor of being multiple people, each of whom "owns" a part of the whole experience, because the whole experience is too much for any one person to tolerate. For the individual with DID, the traumatic events may still be known, but they are "elsewhere known," not known by the whole individual and not experienced as having happened to the whole individual.

As we work with these people, we initially accept their metaphor as we try to meet them where they are and to learn to enter into their emotional world. In accepting the metaphor, we risk allowing it to become concretized, and to mislead us about their world. This error has led to such mistaken interventions as "reparenting," treating an adult patient *as if* he is an infant, using a baby bottle and diapering, or holding an older patient on one's lap. Allowing oneself to concretize the metaphor of multiple individuals in one's body is the first step on a slippery slope to grossly inappropriate behaviors.

It can be difficult to remember that the metaphor is in fact only a metaphor. Often, as we talk with our DID patients, the different "self-states" (the different ways that the patient experiences himself, which are experienced by him as not being the core self) appear. We may see different diction, different body language, different tone of voice, even different vocabulary, all emanating from what is incontestably the same physical body. Any therapist who has treated an individual with DID has likely had the experience of knowing, as the patient enters the room and greets her, that some self-state or alter other than the "host" alter is "in charge of the body" (remember my previous remarks about concretizing the metaphor, and try not to believe that I mean these words concretely. Rather they are the only way I know to describe my own experience). When a thirty year old woman walks in the room carrying her body as a five year old girl would, using the vocabulary and ingenuous tone of a five year old, and asking to do the sorts of things that a five year old would, it is difficult not to believe that a five year old is "in charge" of the thirty year old body. This experience is odd enough that many of us find ourselves skeptical about it, feeling that we have been sucked into a misleading way of talking about the patient's experience, and even feeling crazy ourselves.

I vividly remember an incident when a patient I was treating—a "multiple"—was leaving a therapy session. I asked her if she would be able to keep "the body" safe (because she often experienced her body as not belonging to her). She responded, "It's not my body!" Reflexively, I said, "Well, you live in it, too! You need to keep it safe!" As she walked out of the room, I thought to myself, "What am I doing? This is crazy! I can't treat this woman!" And yet she and I both were speaking about herself and her body in congruence with her internal experience at that moment. To argue that the experience was not "true" would not have done her a service, and by alienating her in that particular self-state would likely have made the therapy (which resulted in her eventual integration and wholeness) impossible.

It is important in such situations to remember that the "different" self-states are in fact only different expressions of a fragmented and incoherent state of being, and that "multiplicity" is a metaphor describing an indescribable state of being. I try always to refer to "the part of you that feels like Toby," to remind us both that the multiplicity is a metaphor. If we do not keep this always in mind, and repeatedly recall it to the patient's mind by our language, we will be colluding with the patient's defense, making the work of therapy more difficult. The language we use can either reinforce the fragmentation of the self or can subtly support whatever sense of wholeness may exist.

Patients with trauma histories also remind us that the emotional resonances of words reflect our history and life experience. Margaret taught me that she was not able to tolerate being told she was good at a task, because when she was a child she had been told she was "a good girl" for not screaming while she was being raped. Polly sometimes had to leave her church services, despite how important her faith was to her, because the service referred to God as "Lord and Master," bringing back memories of the abusive husband who had required her to call him "Master."

Margaret also told me that her only referent for the word "love" was "being hurt," learned because her molester had claimed to love her as he molested her. This led to her being unable to allow herself to love others, because she did not want to hurt anyone else as she had been hurt. It also led to her being unable to allow others to love her, because she did not want to be raped, controlled, humiliated, or hurt in any other way. She did not know that it was possible for intimacy to be nurturing and not hurtful. As Margaret and I learned together about the ways that her childhood had distorted her use of language, she told me that she did not have any way to find meaning in the word "soft": she had no memories of soft touches from her neglectful mother, or soft toys to comfort her, or soft comforting words from anyone.

There were other words that Margaret struggled to hold in her mind. With people who have trouble articulating their feelings, sometimes I will suggest that almost any feeling can be expressed as some combination of "mad, sad, glad, or scared." Margaret was often unable to find words of her own for her feelings, but might be able to recognize and accept words suggested by me (remember that receptive speech precedes expressive speech developmentally). Even when she tried to use these choices, for at least five years she would consistently leave out "scared." Her list of feelings generally included mad, sad, glad, and bad—a clear indication of her profound level of self-criticism, guilt, and shame. She could acknowledge being "bad," feeling guilty or ashamed, more easily than she could acknowledge being scared, because that word brought back her childhood terror.

At other times in her treatment, Margaret and I talked about the need for her to work to hear things with the meanings that others heard, in order to be able to function in relationships with others. At one point, before we both understood why being told she was "good" at something felt so awful to her, we spent most of a session trying to clarify why being praised for her academic work had felt so frightening. Initially, even Margaret thought it was simply because if she admitted she had done well, even more would be expected and she would not be able to do more and to please others. Eventually, in exasperation, I could only say that other people didn't respond as she did to praise; and so she needed to learn to take what they said as they meant it, not as whatever different thing it meant to her. It was hard for her always to remember that not everyone had lived the life she had lived, and that they had different referents for the emotional resonances in many everyday words. Her captivity to the distorted meanings in her own experience prevented her from finding new relationships and supportive connections with others, leaving her alone, lonely, and frightened.

With Margaret I learned again the importance of language, and of defining terms with our patients, of not taking anything at all for granted. Very simple words are often the most difficult, because we learned them before we understood much of the world, and because we believe that everyone understands them. We forget that language reflects early life experience, that what we learn about the world is shaped by how we were treated while we explored it.

Language also reflects current life experience, and with shifts in our patient's ability to understand themselves and to tolerate their own feelings we may see shifts in the language they use. Tom, who came in to treatment saying that he "had anger," was not able to allow himself to be angry enough at others to speak up and defend himself from unjustified attacks. This was clearly related to his early life, when he was expected always to remain subordinate to his critical father, and it had kept him from ever feeling fully successful. As we talked about his anger, and his need to distance himself from it, eventually he was able to say more directly that he "felt anger," and later that he *was* angry, to own the anger. Finally he could make it fully a part of himself, and identify himself as being mad, a more immediate, experience-near way of remembering the experience.

We know that words have power: power to hurt as well as to heal. Many of the people who come for psychotherapeutic treatment have been injured by words, like Dalenberg's "little bit of nothing" (2000). Many more have been injured by actions, like Margaret and Polly and Janet. For all of them, healing can be found when we can find ways to put their experiences into words. When we can say that we have been heard, we are no longer "alone with [our] most dreadful secrets" (Rizzuto, 2003, p. 317).

Speaking of the danger and damage to another who has feelings about it makes it more real, and in some ways more painful than the dissociated, disconnected, "not belonging to me" memory. But it also opens possibilities for changing the current experience, for remembering the event with sorrow rather than only with terror or rage. This in turn allows the memory to be "past," not constantly re-enacted present, such as the flashbacks of PTSD, when the memory overwhelms. When someone hears, understands, and does not hold the victim responsible, it helps the victim to know that he was not at fault, that he did not deserve the abuse. When someone hears and understands and does not look down on the victim, it helps him to feel less ashamed. Finding words for the feelings that accompanied the trauma renders the feelings less overwhelming, because the best way to reduce the intensity of an affect is to verbalize it, and because sorrow shared is sorrow lessened.

More immediately, when *I* hear and understand about my patient's terrible, frightening, painful past, my patient feels less guilty, less shamed, and less overwhelmed. When I am able to help my patient find words for his experience, I can help my patient to manage his feelings about it and to find ways to live with his history without crippling himself through his fear, anger, and grief.

We know that being able to put our feelings into words allows our ego—our conscious mind and the part of our unconscious that deals with reality more than fantasy—to control our behavior and, to some extent, our feelings. It also allows us to distinguish more clearly what is wish or fear and what is reality (Katan, 1961), in the sense that others around us would agree with our perception. I refer to this as recognizing "externally validatable reality," to reflect the idea that fantasies are a part of reality but cannot be confirmed by others, are not "externally validatable." When Janet can talk about her fear that a loving and nurturing person in her life may also want to hurt her, we can begin to sort out what part of that fear is related to her history with her mother and what part may be based on actual events and behaviors of that loving and nurturing person in Janet's life today.

As Janet accepts the idea that others may in fact be loving and nurturing, "motherly" without also being murderous, she must then face the reality that the mother of her childhood may have been loving and nurturing at times, but was also murderous. The grief and rage at this recognition is enormous. Almost always, however, our patients will say that the relief at knowing that you can allow yourself to be loved without simultaneously being afraid of being killed is worth the struggle.

As our patients learn to manage the feelings that accompany traumatic memories, they also begin to be able to allow others into their intensely private world. Many of the people I see with trauma histories have spent much of their life not telling anyone. Sometimes they were afraid they would not be believed; not infrequently, they did tell when they were young children, and were not in fact believed. Sometimes they have been told that what happened was their fault: I'm reminded here of the father who told his wife that the three year old daughter he molested had "come on to" him. To disclose that one was abused, and be believed, and not be blamed, can relieve a lifetime of isolation and separation from others.

As our patients learn to talk about their trauma histories, and to allow others into their frightened, painful, and private world, they begin to allow those others to help them find ways to be safe now. They are able to talk about and explore their fears, finding steps to keep themselves safe and to manage the risks inherent in modern life. They are able to engage in conscious problem-solving, so that they can avoid future dangers rather than only picking up the pieces after the trauma. They can begin, in Kay's words, to "be what I'm supposed to be," instead of hiding from others and from relationships.

As our patients talk about their trauma histories and allow us into their worlds, they also begin to transform the memories in some ways. After telling their story and being met with belief and compassion, each time they remember the trauma after that they may remember the compassion, and perhaps feel very slightly less alone with the pain and the fear.

Fortunately, the majority of the people who come for help through psychotherapy or psychoanalysis are more like Tom or Lily or Aaron than like Margaret or Polly or Janet. Most of my patients have had unhappy lives, and the way they speak about themselves reflects their histories and affects their present lives. For the small percentage with trauma histories—still too many for me to think about without lamenting man's recurrent inhumanity to man!—the effect on their current lives is profound and crippling. For the larger percentage there are no major traumata, but they nevertheless are unhappy and not able to do what they would like with their lives. For both groups, words in psychotherapy and psychoanalysis can offer hope for the future.

NOTE

1. "Trauma" in the specific technical sense used by mental health workers, not in the more global and less intense sense of "unpleasant event."

Chapter Eight

Saying the Unsayable

When Words are Not Enough

How do we take the words that in a dictionary have only content and no emotion and make them serve so many purposes for our interactive lives? We use words to connect to others and to keep them at a distance, to show ourselves to others and to disguise ourselves. And yet the words themselves have no such power. Disconnected from the emotional resonances that live within us, they can do none of those things. In earlier chapters, we explored some of this complex story: how the emotional resonance of our words is acquired in our early relationships, and how the language we use sometimes reflects our internal world by its form as much as by the words we choose.

The way in which our language reflects our internal experience (or does not reflect it) has been a topic of interest in the psychoanalytic literature for many years. In 1956, Loewenstein described for us how emotions become "external as well as internal realities" (p. 463) when put into words. Donnel Stern has written eloquently about words, how we use them, and how they both shape and are shaped by our experience. Originally (DB Stern, 1997) he believed that it is only when we can reflect on our experience verbally that we can formulate it at all; and it is only when we formulate our experience that it becomes meaningful. Prior to formulation, he said then, the meaning of our experience is only *potential.* Before the act of formulation, the experience includes all possible meanings; it is in the act of formulation that the "true" meaning, out of the multitude of possible meanings, actually accrues to the experience. Prior to formulation, all the meanings are simultaneously true, much as Schrodinger's cat, in the quantum physics thought experiment, is simultaneously both alive and dead until one looks into the box to observe which is true.

In later work, Stern's views evolved, and he began (2010) to believe that formulation can be either verbal or nonverbal, that meaning can be found through nonverbal perceptions of self and of Other. When we find meaning and formulation within the transference, he says, we see therapeutic change. Clearly he believes that, although meaning may be found through nonverbal perceptions, it is the verbal exchanges within the therapeutic relationship which carry the transference and countertransference meanings and emotions, sometimes on a nonverbal level. In carrying those meanings and emotions, the verbal exchanges activate the process of therapeutic change, which reaches beyond a strictly verbal understanding. It is our ability to use those verbal exchanges to find and then express the meaning in our experiences that allows psychotherapy to work.

In psychotherapy and psychoanalysis, we work together with our patients to think about their lives, their symptoms, their feelings, and their thoughts. We also think with them about their feelings, their thoughts, and their relationships as those are both described and lived within the therapeutic dyad. To think *about* something in concert with someone else, we need words to convey our thoughts to another person and to hear their thoughts.

When used to convey our thoughts to others and to hear the thoughts of others, words serve to share some part of our experience with the Other, but they are always inadequate to capture the lived experience. Daniel Stern (DN Stern, 1985) has argued that "language . . . causes a split in the experience of the self. It . . . moves relatedness onto the impersonal, abstract level intrinsic to language and away from the personal, immediate level. . . ." (p. 163). He sees the "impersonal, abstract level" of language as a layer of experience that resides alongside the nonverbal layer but remains separate from it to an important degree. That is, once the child begins to speak, the powerful organizing capacities of language make sensorimotor modes of organizing experience—touch and smell and taste and movement—less immediate. Speaking, then, allows us to share our experience with others but also requires us to step back from the immediacy of it. He maintains that the subtleties of self-experience and interpersonal experience are lost in the shift to language, initially as verbalization takes hold in early life, and then forever after. For Daniel Stern, nonverbal experience is not simply unconnected to or disconnected from the verbal realm. Its very accessibility to "linear" language is dubious. And maturation and development are responsible for the disconnection, as a consequence of language acquisition.

And yet Stern also says that "words have an existence, a life of their own that permits language to transcend lived experience and to be generative" (p. 168–69). In his view, implicit relational knowing, a nonverbal way of knowing, exists parallel to and interacts with the explicit language-based way of knowing. The emergence of language

> forces a space between interpersonal experience as lived and as represent-ed...but also with language, infants for the first time can share their personal experience of the world with others, including 'being with' others in intimacy, isolation, loneliness, fear, awe, and love. (DN Stern, 1985, pg. 182)

"Being with" others as we share our experience of the world with them adds to the memory of the lived experience, changing it in ways that remembering it alone, either nonverbally or verbally, does not. Each time we remember an experience we remember it at least very slightly differently, because the new memory now includes the associations considered with the previous memo-ry. When we have shared the memory with someone else, the memory is also shaped by the words we used to share it; our memory of the conversation about the memory; the reaction of the Other when we shared our memory; and our memory of interactions with the Other about the original memory. When we remember both what happened to us *and* that we told someone else about it, we are no longer alone with the memory: it is past and no longer a visceral "here-and-now" experience. It is this reworking and transformation of the memory, so that one is no longer alone with it, that is one helpful element for individuals with histories of trauma. When Janet in chapter 7 remembers the terrible abuse she suffered, she now also remembers that someone else knows about it and hurts for and with her, and she is less alone in at least some small measure. Transforming the memory in this way allows her to make it a memory, rather than as the immediate and terrifying reliving of a flashback.

I am unsatisfied with Stern's assertion that language "drives a wedge between two simultaneous forms of interpersonal experience: as it is lived and as it is verbally represented" (DN Stern, 1985, p. 192). Although it feels true to me, it also feels incomplete: on the level of *implicit* knowing, the *explicit* statement cannot stand without qualification. I know that words can never accurately reflect the entirety of the internal experience. We do not tell about what happened in all its complexity: we tell about what we remember, what we have understood, what sense we have made of the experience. If we cannot make sense of it, we may not be able to talk about it, much as I was unable to talk comprehensibly about Lily, from chapter 3, until I was able to make some sense of my experience with her.

It is also true that words do create some distance from our emotions, and this effect is often helpful both in life and in the psychotherapeutic process: the not-so-simple act of putting one's feelings into words creates at least a small degree of intellectualization, which helps one to step back from and observe the emotion, rather than being overwhelmed by it. When Janet felt she was drowning in fear we found words to express her terror, guilt, and shame. The words served as a lifeline so that she could keep her head above water until she could find other ways to manage the sense of being over-whelmed by her feelings. The slight step back from the feelings makes the telling within the therapeutic dyad more than simply a retraumatization for our patients. As we use our words to contain the emotions, to create distance from them, we also use the words to clarify and sharpen the emotions. In talking about the emotions we are no longer alone with them, and we experi-ence them anew in attenuated and less overwhelming form.

We can use language defensively, to take refuge in the words that contain and inhibit the affective reality of the experience, avoiding the emotional resonances of our words so as to avoid the emotions associated with our experience. Some patients show no emotion at all in describing overwhelm-ing life experiences, or show emotions that are incongruous to the events, as when they giggle while talking about a life-threatening illness. When we observe this, we know that these people are avoiding the emotional reality of the event; and most likely the way they talk about that event helps them to set the feelings aside.

Language also, however, allows us to relive a part of the original experi-ence; to share some part of the experience with others; and to find new ways of understanding what the experience means. The original experience can never be repeated, and cannot be shared with others. We can remember it, often using words to do so; and we can share it with others, most often using words to do so. Language establishes a mode of thinking about experience that allows us to step back and observe our experience *as well as* to experi-ence it partially again in memory, and the two modes of reflection may enrich each other. As I consider this possibility, I see an image of a braided cable, with the two modes of experience intertwined and combining to make something stronger than either component alone. The two separate modes of experience also influence each other, and are influenced by each other: when Dr. Dalenberg and her patient, in chapter 7, talked about what it meant to be "a little bit of nothing," the young girl created a new experience that incorpo-rated *both* the memory of her father's scorn *and* the memory of Dr. Dalen-berg's compassion and concern. This new, integrated experience allowed her to choose how to hear the words. The "braided cable" has become a new substance, which is more than the sum of its parts. Perhaps we lose some-thing when we find words for our experiences. But in becoming able to think about it, and to remember and share it with others, we gain a great deal.

The words alone, of course, are never enough. Whether our patients in-tend it or not, they add emotional nuances to the simple words they speak by the way they speak those words. Tone of voice is one of the most important: think about the sentence "I'm coming" as it is said in an anticipatory way, expressing eagerness to arrive; an angry way, expressing irritation or exasperation; a fearful way, expressing anxiety or even terror. The same words may convey multiple meanings depending on tone of voice. An ironic or sarcastic tone will contradict the superficial meaning of the words, setting the *semantic* content in opposition to the *communicated* content. Even in electronic communication, which by definition has no "tone of voice," conventions have developed to convey tone: emoticons such as :) for a smile, or "LOL" (laughing out loud) to convey humorous intent, or all capitals for shouting.

Diction, relaxed or clipped or drawling, also adds to the emotional resonance of the words. The "mother tongue" that emerges when I am with a distressed patient, with my Texas accent, drawling and dropping my g's, is the soothing resonance of my own infancy, captured in the nonverbal aspects of my voice and person. When I am irritated or angry, I speak more rapidly, sharply, with an edge that conveys the irritation. It is most likely impossible to speak meaningfully if one attends only to the meaning of the words without some nonverbal cues: even reading dialogue in a play or a book, words written by others, tends to take on a rhythm and tone related to conveyed emotions unless the words are meaningless to us.

The nonverbal ways of conveying meaning are critical to making sense when we speak, because the simple content of our words is often entirely inadequate. I find myself, with my patients, at times saying in frustration that "there aren't any good words for what I mean!" I struggle to find words that will share the simultaneous emotional and intellectual understanding of how they defend themselves from emotional pain and conflict. I struggle even more to find words for that understanding that are meaningful and not "loaded" in unfortunate ways—words that do not cause even more emotional pain and conflict. At those times, I may resort to sharing my own associative paths. As Joseph tells me about his struggles to make himself complete an assignment at work, in my reverie I remember the fourth grader whose parents stood over him angrily every day while he was unable to finish his math homework. When I bring that association into the room, we both remember the anguish of that fourth grader, which is close cousin to the anguish of Joseph at 40. This association tells Joseph that I recognize and understand his current pain, as well as suggesting a new way to think about the current problems at work.

At other times when I cannot find words to express my thoughts, I may resort to similes or metaphors. In talking about the effects of medications to help contain emotional overload, I may say that a particular medication "turns down the volume" of the anxiety, so that my patient can tolerate it and examine it. Or I may describe an image of a cup that holds all the emotional tension in our lives, both pleasant and unpleasant, and when the cup overflows because of life events or internal tension, symptoms of depression or anxiety or anger appear. With medication, we may be able either to enlarge the cup, or to reduce the level of the tension, so that the cup does not overflow. Neither of these figures of speech describes anything like what the medication actually does biologically. But it describes what the medication has to offer in ways that are emotionally meaningful to my patients, which they can use to understand why we are doing what we are doing in their treatment.

We use language to share our thoughts and feelings with others, and to share our understanding of their thoughts and feelings. In psychotherapy, we also use language to acknowledge our patient's primary process fantasies, wishes, and dreams and to bring them together with the secondary process limitations of external reality": Only language can bring together the conscious verbal knowing of secondary process and the doing, feeling, and being of primary process" (Vivona, 2003, p. 55). We may use logical, secondary process words to evoke primary process emotion and sensorimotor experience ("Love is a rose"), as well as beginning with sensorimotor experience and bringing it to logical secondary process thought through words ("My heart was in my throat"). In bridging the gap between the two modes of experience, metaphor provides a critical span (note here the use of metaphor to convey a complex idea)."The embracing capacities of language have been conceptualized within psychoanalysis as the particular purview of metaphor, that figure of speech whose potential to induce transformative intrapsychic and interpersonal connections has been illuminated" (Vivona, 2003, p. 55). Because of the emotional histories of our words, when they are used in metaphors to form connections with early emotion-laden experiences, the metaphor becomes "the funnel through which a history of overwhelming sensation, affectivity, and states of confusion can be poured, shaped, and articulated" (Wilson and Weinstein, 1992, p. 742) (another, different metaphor, expressing a different aspect of the process).

Metaphors allow us to make connections between familiar and unfamiliar thoughts, between current sensations and emotions and past events and sensations. Because they make connections between disparate thoughts on multiple levels, as well as disparate experiences, they also allow us to open new possibilities for being. When we can find metaphors for the ineffable aspects of life, it becomes possible to talk about them rather than to re-enact them, and we can learn about previously unrecognized facets of ourselves.

When we attend to the differences as well as the similarities between the two parts of the metaphor, we can expand our emotional experience even more. But if we take the metaphor too far, we may believe that the experience is fully understood and expressed and then we shut off new thoughts or feelings about the original experience. If we think that the similarities expressed by the metaphor are all that matters, and do not recognize that the comparison eventually fails, we run the risk of concretizing it: as when individuals with dissociative identity disorder are responded to as if they are truly several different people, rather than one person with several different and disconnected experiences of themselves.

Similes and analogies, of course, are closely related to metaphors, and share some of their power. The immediacy and complexity of the metaphor brings power and intensity to the comparison of past and present. Similes, which specifically state that the comparison is *as if,* emphasize the disconnection between language and lived experience, moving us away from the personal, immediate level evoked by the metaphor's "It *is.*" "Love is a rose" is a much more powerful statement emotionally than "love is like a rose," although the content of each is similar. The simile also limits the comparison between the unlike elements being examined. Where a metaphor insists that we find other ways in which the comparison is true, the simile stops with the stated likeness. It does not invite us to extend the comparison, or to broaden our reactions beyond the stated partial likeness.

In therapy, we may use a simile rather than a metaphor when the patient is on the verge of being overwhelmed by the emotion lurking in the background of the conversation. If Janet tells me that it is dangerous to let me close, I will reframe it within a few sentences as "You *feel* like it is dangerous..." Introducing the "danger" as a simile takes a step back from the metaphorical danger, which to Janet does not feel at all metaphorical, but feels like the same danger that she was in when mother tried to murder her. It introduces the limits of the comparison, and so brings a breath of present-day reality— that I am as safe as anyone can be in her life—to the conversation. In my own practice, I also tend to use similes when I am unsure about the emotional connection. A metaphor invites our acknowledgement of likeness at multiple levels, while a simile brings less power to the emotional association because it refers to only a limited sort of likeness. The limits to the comparison allow my patient to reject it more easily if it is incorrect or poorly timed. For instance, I might tell a male patient that he feels as if he's a little boy who has failed to please his father, rather than saying that he feels four years old, again failing to please his father. This tentativeness allows some distance, so that if he is not yet ready to know that he is reliving that experience, the awareness is not forced on him.

Analogies also offer comparisons between like and unlike experiences or objects, and in some ways move even further toward the abstract intellectualized perspective. Analogies, like metaphors, present an invitation to find previously unrecognized ways in which the current experience and the analogic experience are alike. Occasionally I will tell a new patient that the first stages of psychotherapy are in some ways like walking in a dark wood: we walk in darkness (talk without knowing where we are going, as they say whatever comes to mind) until we run into a tree (discover an insight). We then put up a light (develop an insight), which shows us some of the territory to be explored (answers to old questions as well as new questions to consider). After we have explored the new territory, we venture into more darkness, until we run into another tree, and put up another light. This analogy conveys the apparent aimlessness of the initial exploration, helping us both to tolerate not having immediate solutions to my patient's distress. It offers hope for insight and future awareness, and warns about the possible painfulness of those insights. It also offers the possibility of pursuing questions about the analogy that may be relevant to the therapy: who is leading the wandering? What if we find a clear path when we put up the light? Can the lights go out, and cease to be useful? Do we know if there are dangerous animals in the woods?

In a metaphor, because it finds multiple levels of similarity between the two elements compared and asserts identity between them, the momentum of the thought is in the direction of finding more similarities. The metaphor almost insists on more. The analogy also often will find multiple levels of similarity, but explicitly expects the comparison to fail, so that the pressure to find more points of likeness is less. Even in its failing the analogy is useful, as it becomes the "*disanalogy* which enables us to preserve what was right about the analogy" (Oppenheimer, 1956, p. 132). Exploring how the analogy fails allows us to identify what is important in the issue under discussion, and may offer guides to new analogies (or metaphors or similes) that illuminate new ways of thinking about the issue.

Of course we also find the emotional power of metaphor and simile outside of psychotherapy and psychoanalysis. Metaphors that have migrated from technical literature to general vocabulary offer new ways of thinking about and describing our experiences. Since the 1960s, it has been possible and meaningful to say that one has a "laser focus" on a topic, to express intense and tightly limited attention. The advent of computers, and the language of computers, has brought many new words and metaphors to our language, offering both new vocabulary and new ways of thinking about the connections and interconnections in society. The "worldwide web" is itself a metaphor that conveys both the interconnectedness and the "stickiness" (sometimes unwanted connections, as when one's computer is hacked) of the internet. Of particular interest to people who deal with neurology and psychology is the distinction between software and hardware, a high tech way of talking about our attempts to determine what is nature (hardware or biology) and what is nurture (software or "programming"). When we use these new terms to speak about our experiences, without noticing we are introducing new possibilities to our thinking about those experiences.

Language and words are so much a part of our lives that for the most part we don't notice them. DB Stern (2012) suggests "that there is very little in our world that is not at least *touched* by language in a meaningful way. A great deal of the experience we describe as both meaningful and nonverbal, perhaps even all of it, is *made* meaningful by its relation to language."

Dance, for instance, is differentiated by its label from all other sorts of movement, many of which have no meaning, only function. A reaching out to an object, for instance, in "real life" may have no meaning except the function of taking the object, where in dance it has a meaning that contributes to the total meaning in the dance.

Nonverbal forms of communication—music, art, dance—all are ways to convey emotions and emotional meanings to others. In our viewing or participating in these activities, the visceral sensorimotor reaction is very "experience-near." They are all "thing-expressions" of emotion: they are visible, can be observed by more than one person, and so are not only internal experiences. But they communicate by evoking an experience and avoiding the words that would elicit a more secondary process, conscious consideration of meaning.

Poetry also acts by evoking emotions, but because it uses words to do so, the conscious secondary process thought that is required to understand the words involves that part of our perceptual/cognitive/affective processing "apparatus." In the same way that I had to "translate" Kay's art, in chapter 1, into a visual metaphor so that I could think about it analytically, poetry requires us to use the verbal parts of our brains to consider the poem. Poetry, however, merges the primary process feelings with the secondary process thinking-about, which brings the emotions closer to the sort of secondary process thought that we use most of the time to interact with others, evoking both implicit and explicit modes of reflection.

Literature that focuses on conveying emotion, either in prose or in poetry, plays a powerful role in our cultures and our lives. Often we can only think of quoting some playwright or author when we need to make a powerful point, because we cannot find our own words: "Poetry is the way we help give name to the nameless so it can be thought" (Lorde, 1984). In poetry, and in lyric prose, the semantic content of the words serves primarily to evoke emotions, to recall experiences, to create a new and not essentially verbal experience. "What if a much of a which of a wind" (e.e. cummings, 1926, p. 401) cannot be said to have any semantic content that can be rendered in other words: but the poem itself evokes a strong emotional reaction that leads me to want to read it multiple times. Another poem by cummings, "my father moved through dooms of love/through sames of am through haves of give" (1926, pp. 373–375) can fairly reliably bring me to tears, even though I am completely unable to tell you what it means semantically.

Poets and playwrights use words to evoke emotional reactions in us. In order to share those reactions with others, we must find a way to express ourselves. And if we want to communicate more than the simple existence of the emotion, the way we have to do this is with words. As we try to share our reactions with others, we move at least a slight distance away from the primal intensity of the emotion, because finding words to reflect the internal reality introduces the secondary process limitations. The patient who brought music to share with me wanted me to know how she felt: but even if the music had communicated to me as it did to her, it would have told me only the broadest outlines of her feelings. We would not have been able to talk about the intensity of the grief, or fear, or anger, or joy, or about the source of the emotion. Nonverbal modes of expression convey emotions without a content that can be thought about, whereas verbal modes of expression lend themselves to both emotion and to conscious thought.

At the beginning of this chapter, I remarked that words serve both to connect us to others and to protect us from being too close, they allow us to both express and conceal our emotions, to show others about ourselves and protect our secrets. Ultimately, words are how we construct bridges between ourselves and others, and the way we use our words determines how easily the bridges may be crossed—perhaps whether there is a troll hiding under the bridge to prevent passage.

Chapter Nine

Why Do Words Matter?

We know that words help us to think, to communicate, to connect with others. In much of our life, words are the foundation of thought. But there certainly are other ways to process our world, to take in information and to arrive at conclusions. To call this implicit process "thinking" is in some ways incorrect, and for many people the word "thinking" implies a conscious process. For our purposes here, I would ask you to accept the "controlled inaccuracy" of using the word "thinking" as a first approximation, leaving discussions of what is true thinking and what is some other form of knowing and understanding ourselves for another day.

If we accept the inherent sloppiness of using a term that does not quite fit what we are considering, it seems apparent that infants think before they have words to think with: in the first days and weeks of life they are already gathering information about their world, creating hypotheses (necessarily nonverbal) about what the sounds and movements around them might mean. As adults, we "think" implicitly when we do familiar things such as tie a knot: if we stop to think about it consciously, we may forget what we are doing because the conscious verbal thinking interferes with the unconscious, implicit, somatic thinking. I believe that in Kay's treatment, described in chapter 1, she was thinking in pictures (as does Temple Grandin) because she did not have words for her inner self with which she could think about herself.

Nonverbal thinking is a component of what happens in psychotherapy when I make an interpretation: I suggest to my patient that his behavior or his words reveal some particular conflict or thought. The content of the interpretation is important, because it must make sense and be logical. But whether it is *correct* is another issue: it is entirely possible that my patient will understand what I am saying, that he will see why I made the suggestion, but he will know, in some ineffable nonverbal way, that it is incorrect. When I am correct, the "aha experience" of recognizing my correctness is a type of thinking, even though it does not rely on words for the "aha." At other times I will share a thought that did not come from verbal conscious thinking-through, but that appeared in my reverie for reasons that I cannot name. In that case, I might say, "I have no idea where this idea comes from, but I thought just now about. . . ." My associational path, shared through words with my patient, is the outcome of the nonverbal processes that led to the intervention.

Words are not the only way we have to think (or to do whatever verb might accurately reflect this process), but they do make it possible to think in an interpersonal world. As Litowitz tells us (2012), "It is only through language . . . that our inner world, shaped through communicational exchanges with others, can be brought into communication with others, now sharable in a way that can be discussed (i.e., brought into joint attention and reference), negotiated, and altered" (p. 271). Without words, we have no clear way to share our thoughts with others, to move them out of the confines of our own head into the heads of others where they can be added to and refined. Without words we cannot think-with others, we cannot add their experience to our own and find meanings and thoughts that are new to us. When we cannot think-with, our ability to use the power of shared effort in our tasks is limited.

Without words our ability to join the community of others is also limited. Nacht (1963) tells us that "the communication necessary for a relationship is established by the use of words" (p. 335). With words, we join with others, sharing our thoughts and perhaps our feelings, and we make ourselves known to them. Words link us to others. As we link to others, and make ourselves known to them, we also learn to know ourselves. Putting our thoughts and feelings into words allows us to share them with others, and being clear for others as we express ourselves makes it possible for us to be more clear in our private thoughts.

Finding words for our thoughts often coalesces them, leading us to make new connections and find new insights. Many of us use this aspect of language in order to discover what we think by writing. My own writing has always been at least in part to clarify my thoughts, and the professional writing I have done has been generally about patients or clinical situations that were particularly troublesome to me. In the process of writing, of describing patients or clinical dilemmas to others, I "discover" what seems most important to me about the dilemma and I find ways of thinking more clearly about it. In chapter 3, when I described the chaos of Lily's entry into treatment, I reported my unsuccessful efforts to find a way to articulate what was happening. It was only as I was able finally to describe my own experience with Lily through writing it that I became able to articulate what I understood of Lily's experience as she brought it to me. That in turn allowed me to share that understanding with Lily, and then to help her to bring order to her own experience and to articulate it.

In writing this book, I recognized this particular aspect of finding words for my thoughts. Originally, when friends asked what I was writing about, I was unable to describe the book briefly. I had in mind a series of vignettes that were only vaguely linked but that all seemed to me to express some element of the ways that language was important in my work, and the ways that various failures of language in my work had caught my attention. I remembered Kay and Susan, whom I described in chapters 1 and 2; I thought about Barbara, from chapter 3, and the experience of working psychoanalytically with people for whom English is not the first language. I remembered my experiences over the years with children who had learning disabilities affecting their language, and the various ways that their ability to manage themselves had been compromised; I thought about the patients I knew whose traumatic histories had interfered with their ability to speak about themselves in various ways, or for whom words had acquired distorted meanings. I remembered my personal experiences with a psychoanalytic writing program (New Directions, at the Washington Center for Psychoanalysis), where I learned to write comprehensibly rather than in a dense and impenetrable jargon, and where I observed others struggling to improve their own writing. In that program I first observed how often the other writers in the program would turn to poetry when they were unable to find in prose the feelings that they were trying to capture.

Most of these scattered fragments of thoughts had been "present" with me for many years, but I had never pulled them together in any organized way. After I was offered a contract to write a book about language and psychotherapy, based on those disconnected ideas, I began trying to find a way to communicate to others what I believed I had learned. My first efforts were painfully dense, jargon-filled, and I am sure boring. But as I spoke with friends, family, and colleagues about my thoughts and my efforts, I began to understand that I could lead others into the intrigue of these ideas the same way I had discovered it: by describing Kay, and Susan, and the clinical experiences which had caught my attention. And as I did that, and began putting my vague ideas on paper, I worked to flesh them out and find what I could in the analytic literature to help me explore them. With this effort, my thoughts evolved and expanded to include other issues and to link the fragments of thoughts. Today, when I look back over notes I had made several years ago about these issues, the notes seem distant and disconnected from where I have arrived in my thinking.

My efforts to find ways to write clearly, concisely, and interestingly about these issues have spawned new ideas and new directions of thought, and some of the things I have written about here would never have occurred to me before I began the book. Putting thoughts into words in order to share them with others has helped me not only to know what I think, but to have new thoughts.

Putting thoughts into words in order to share them with others is of course not exclusively positive. It is problematic when we forget that the words are only a distant shadow of the experience. If we take words as truth rather than as partial expressions of experience, we turn away from the honest experience, and disjunctions and damage occur in our attempts to interact with others. The damage is particularly severe when the error is committed by caretakers, such as parents, teachers, or therapists, if the one being cared for accepts the confusion of word and truth. When mother says, "You're killing me!" and the child believes it as literal truth, the child may respond by killing himself, emotionally if not physically, so as to preserve mother's life.

At other times, finding verbal expression for our experiences may have the same effect as opening the box where Schrodinger's quantum hypothesis cat resides, both alive and dead: for the cat, once we open the box it is *either* alive or dead, no longer both. Once we find coherent expression for our thoughts, we lose sight of the possibilities not expressed. Opening the box has limited us to only one, to the particular associational path which we have chosen to put into words. When we forget that we are letting go of other associations, we move away from all the possibilities that might have appeared if we had verbalized them differently, or if we had chosen a different part of the thought to emphasize.

I have been aware in writing this book of the possibility that I might lose some valuable insights and ideas as I struggled to find the shape of what I wanted to say. At times an early draft of a particular chapter was chaotic, disorganized, and difficult to read because I was trying not to let go of all the various paths which I might take. Bringing order to the chaos, and finding links between the various disconnected thoughts without losing most of them, was an important part of the process of deciding how to share my ideas with others through this book.

My struggle to think about and verbalize my thoughts, so that others might read them and think more deeply on these issues, has also allowed me to know more about myself and my own relationship to the matters I discuss here. I have considered myself to be primarily a scientist, interested in the theory behind the work I do. In writing this book, I have realized that I am in fact primarily interested in praxis, the ways that we translate theory into our activity in the consulting room with our patients. Theory and the underlying science are important but not sufficient to the work, as language is necessary but not sufficient in communicating fully about thoughts, feelings, and self with others.

One of the problems I experienced as I wrote was in the nature of language itself. In trying to write about the subtle nuances and shadings that we can convey in language, we have to use the language itself to convey those nuances, and that language itself can distort what we are trying to say. A very early version of chapter 2, from my days as a new therapist, was written in a self-consciously professional voice, with the same content as the current version, but much less experience-near and much less easy to read. As I tried to convey the *experience* of working with Susan, more than the intellectual understanding of the work, the various revisions moved more and more toward what has appeared here. I also recognized this at work in Vivona's 2012 paper and the various commentaries on it: each by a different writer, each with a different voice, and each voice moving the reader to different conclusions (Bucci; Fonagy; Litowitz; DN Stern; and Vivona: all from 2012 and all cited separately). Vivona herself, in her response to the commentaries, remarks that she chose to use the word "nonverbal" "to do something more than denote its standard definition, in particular to propel an emphatic argument. . . ."She adds that use of terms such as "somatic" ". . . does not set up an automatic opposition of verbal and experiential modes of being" and thus "does not necessarily foreclose our thinking about verbal involvements in lived experience" (p. 305). Reading the paper, the commentaries on it, and her response to the commentaries is a lesson in how the words we choose can constrict our thinking without our noticing.

The words we choose, and the nuances they convey, can also result in "tonal" differences in what is expressed. I am aware that various chapters of this book have very different voices, for different reasons. My voice in chapter 7, on speaking the unspeakable, is often more distant and intellectualized than in other chapters, undoubtedly because the emotional reality of working with terribly traumatized individuals is difficult to tolerate when there is no interpersonal need. In chapter 5, which describes the acquisition of language, my voice again is more distant and less experience-near, because I am describing something I *know* rather than something I *remember*. I have never had a child, and cannot bring those emotional resonances to the descriptions of the events. At the same time, I have had relationships with children who mattered to me—relatives as well as patients—and so the descriptions are likely not entirely without echoes of the memories evoked by the descriptions.

All these thoughts matter because as we write, and as we find words with which to share our thoughts, we are reaching out to others in our world. Any verbalized thought must of necessity have an audience. We are, at the least, communicating with ourselves, with the internal auditor who shapes and censors our conscious thought. We learned to find words to communicate with others within our early relationships, and the nature of those early relationships has shaped how we use our language. Horton (1984) has clearly described the ways in which distorted relationships distort language: growing up in a comfortless, disorganized family creates individuals with disorganized language who are unable to use it to comfort themselves or others. Their speech is "not infused with the vitality of human relatedness" (p. 177), and the relationships which rely on that language are disorganized or dysfunctional in various ways. We speak to others in the world today expecting them to hear us as those in our early lives would have heard us.

Whenever we speak, we reach out to our audience, hoping to share our thoughts and feelings, and ultimately ourselves, with them. Language is the embodiment of a wish to not be alone in the world, the wish to connect with others. Most of my patients come to me because their ability to live in a relational world has been compromised in some way, in their experiences with others or in their experiences within themselves, their feelings and thoughts. Often they are unable to manage the intense emotions which drive their maladaptive behaviors, in part because they have no way to think about those emotions clearly. As we work together to help them to think more clearly about their emotions and to live successfully in a relational world, language is a fundamental tool because living in a relational world requires it.

As this book evolved, I began to look for possible metaphors which would allow us to find new ways to think of our work in psychotherapy and psychoanalysis, and lead us to new ways to help our patients. I came to imagine psychoanalysts and psychotherapists as "master interpreters," whose task is to understand what our patients are saying, and to translate. We must use their idiosyncratic "language"—the concepts and emotions that underlie their behaviors—to help them recognize themselves and understand how and why they feel what they feel and live their lives as they do.

We translate our patients first to ourselves, and then to themselves: we interpret the behaviors of others to them, and help them see (hear?) how and why others misunderstand their intent, or how they misunderstand the intentions of others. In family therapy, or in considering the families of our patients, we help them to identify the "family language" that binds the family together, as well as the "language" that prevents them from being closer.

Fonagy (2012) writes that "the particular mystery of language as part of the therapeutic process is the almost infinite range of ideational frames that can bring relief: words about the past, about the present, of thoughts and of feelings, about self-states and about relationships, outside and inside the consulting room, about the world and about the person, about attachment figures and about those for whom one hardly has emotion at all" (p. 293). I would modify that thought only slightly, to suggest that the "particular mystery" of language and words in the therapeutic process is the way in which they allow us to link all those ideational frames, and to translate one into another. As we translate feelings into thoughts, or ideas about self-states into actions within relationships, we connect the fragments of self and of our representational world. We connect ourselves inside the consulting room to the world outside, the past to the present, our individual selves to the collective world, all at least in part through the ways in which we use words.

I have in this book barely begun to describe the remarkable flexibility and possibilities of language for both harm and for healing. I hope that the pieces of the puzzle presented here will allow others to pick up the puzzle box and find new pieces, providing new connections and new ways to explore and express ourselves.

Bibliography

Amati-Mehler, J., Argentieri, S., & Canestri, J. (1990). The babel of the unconscious. *International Journal of Psycho-Analysis, 71*, 569–583.

Barth, F.D. (1998). Speaking of feelings: Affects, language, and psychoanalysis. *Psychoanalytic Dialogues, 8*, 685–705.

Bollas, C. (1987). *The Shadow of the Object.* New York: Columbia University Press.

Brinich, P.M. (1981). Application of the Metapsychological Profile to the assessment of deaf children. *Psychoanalytic Study of the Child, 36*, 3–32.

Bromberg, P. (1994). "Speak! That I may see you": Some reflections on dissociation, reality, and psychoanalytic listening. *Psychoanalytic Dialogues, 4*, 517–547.

Bucci, W. (2012). Is there language disconnected from sensory/bodily experience in speech or thought? Commentary on Vivona. *Journal of the American Psychoanalytic Association, 60*, 275–285.

Call, J.D. (1980). Some prelinguistic aspects of language development. *Journal of the American Psychoanalytic Association, 28*, 259–289.

Chefetz, R.A. (2000). Dysregulation as a way of life. *Journal of the American Academy of Psychoanalysis, 28*, 289–303.

Chomsky, N. (1965). *Aspects of the Theory of Syntax.* Cambridge, MA: MIT Press.

cummings, e.e. (1926). *e.e. cummings: Poems, 1923–54.* New York: Harcourt, Brace, and World.

Curtiss, S. (1977). *Genie: A Psycholinguistic Study of a Modern–Day "Wild Child."* London: Academic Press

Dalenberg, C. (2000). *Countertransference and the Treatment of Trauma.* Washington, DC: American Psychological Association.

Davis, K. (1947). Final note on a case of extreme isolation. *American Journal of Sociology, 52*, 554–565.

DeCasper, A.J. & Spence, J.M. (1986). Prenatal maternal speech influences newborns' perception of speech sounds. *Infant Behavior and Development, 9*, 133–150.

Edgcumbe, R.M. (1981). Toward a developmental line for the acquisition of language. *Psychoanalytic Study of the Child, 36*, 71–103.

Etezady, M.H. (2011). Neurotic inhibitions of play. In *Play and Playfulness: Developmental, Cultural, and Clinical Aspects*, p. 51–68. Ed. M. C. Akhtar. Lanham, MD: Jason Aronson Books.

Etezady, M. H., & Davis, M. (Eds.). (2012). *Keeping Your Child's Mind in Mind: Perspectives on Reflective Parenting.* Lanham, MD: Jason Aronson Press.

Fernald, A. (1993). Approval and disapproval: Infant responsiveness to vocal affect in familiar and unfamiliar languages. *Child Development, 64*, 657–667.

Fonagy, P. (2012). Does it matter if there is a nonverbal period of development: On the infant's understanding the social world and its implications for psychoanalytic therapy. *Journal of the American Psychoanalytic Association, 60*, 287–296.

Fonagy, P., Gergely, G., Jurist, E., & Target, M. (2005). *Affect Regulation, Mentalization, and the Development of the Self.* New York: Other Press.

Fraiberg, S. (1968). Parallel and divergent patterns in blind and sighted infants. *Psychoanalytic Study of the Child, 23,* 264–300.

Fraiberg, S. & Adelson, E. (1973).Self–representation in language and play: Observations of blind children. *Psychoanalytic Quarterly, 42,* 539–562.

Freedman, D.A. (1981). The effect of sensory and other deficits in children on their experience of people. *Journal of the American Psychoanalytic Association, 29,* 831–867.

Freedman, D.A. & Hansen, D.B. (1985). The influence of early deficits on later development. *Journal of the American Psychoanalytic Association, 33,* 631–644.

Freud, A. (1969). Comments on psychic trauma. In *Writings of Anna Freud, v. V: Research at the Hampstead Child Therapy Clinic and Other Papers, 1956–65.* New York: International Universities Press, pp. 221–241.

Freud, A. in collaboration with D. Burlingham. (1973). Five types of air raid anxiety. In *Writings of Anna Freud, v. III: Infants Without Families, Reports on the Hampstead Nurseries, 1939–1945.* New York: International Universities Press, pp. 163–172.

Gedo, J. (1996). *The Languages of Psychoanalysis.* Hillsdale, NJ: The Analytic Press.

Grandin, T. (1995, 2006). *Thinking in Pictures and Other Reports from My Life with Autism.* NY: Vintage Books.

Horton, P.C. (1984). Language, solace, and transitional relatedness. *Psychoanalytic Study of the Child, 39,* 167–194.

Joliffe, T., Lakesdown, R., & Robinson, C. (1992).Autism, a personal account. *Communication, 26,* 12–19.

Katan, A. (1961). Some thoughts about the role of verbalization in early childhood. *Psychoanalytic Study of the Child, 16,*184–188.

Kisilevsky, B.S., Hains, S.M., Lee, K., Xie, S., Huang, H., Ye, H.H., Zhang, K., & Wang, Z. (2003). Effects of experience on fetal voice recognition. *Psychological Science, 14,* 220–224.

Krapf, E. (1955). The choice of language in polyglot psychoanalysis. *The Psychoanalytic Quarterly, 24,* 343–357.

Krystal, H. (1988). *Integration and Self Healing: Affect, Trauma, Alexithymia.* Hillside, NJ: The Analytic Press.

Lewis, C.S. (1950).*The Lion, the Witch, and the Wardrobe.* New York: Harper Collins.

Lewis, M. (1977). Language, cognitive development, and personality. *Journal of the American Academy of Child Psychiatry, 16,* 646–661.

Liebal, I., Behne, T., Carpenter, M., & Tomasello, M. (2009). Infants use shared experience to interpret pointing gestures. *Developmental Science,* 12, 264–271.

Liszowski, U., Carpenter, M. & Tomasello, M. (2008). Twelve–month–olds communicate helpfully and appropriately for knowledgeable and ignorant partners. *Cognition, 108,* 732–739.

Litowitz, B.E. (2011). From dyad to dialogue: Language and the early relationship in American psychoanalytic theory. *Journal of the American Psychoanalytic Association, 59,* 483–507.

Litowitz, B.E. (2012). Why this question? Commentary on Vivona. *Journal of the American Psychoanalytic Association, 60,* 267–274.

Loewald, H.W. (1980).Primary process, secondary process, and language. In *Papers on Psychoanalysis* (pp. 178–206). New Haven, CT: Yale University Press. (Original work published 1978).

Loewenstein, R.M. (1956).Some remarks on the role of speech in psycho–analytic technique. *International Journal of Psycho–Analysis, 37,* 460–468.

Lorde, A. (1984). "Poetry Is Not a Luxury." *Sister Outsider: Essays and Speeches.* Freedom, CA: Crossing Press. pp. 36–39.

Mahler, M., Pine, F., & Bergman, A. (1975). *The Psychological Birth of the Human Infant: Symbiosis and Individuation.* New York: Basic Books.

Mason, M.K. (1942). Learning to speak after six and one half years of silence. *Journal of Speech and Hearing Disorders, 7,* 295–304.

Meltzoff, A.N. & Brooks, R. (2009). The role of gaze following in early word learning. In J. Colombo, P. McCardle, & L. Freund (Eds.), *Infant Pathways to Language: Methods, Models, and Research Directions.* New York: Psychology Press, pp. 169–194.

Mills, A. (1993).Visual handicap. In D. Bishop & K. Mogford (Eds.), *Language Development in Exceptional Circumstances.* Hillsdale, NJ: Lawrence Erlbaum Associates. pp. 150–76.

Nacht, S. (1963). The non–verbal relationship in psychoanalytic treatment. *International Journal of Psychoanalysis, 44,* 334–338.

National Institute of Neurological Disorders and Stroke (2005). Asperger syndrome fact sheet. Retrieved from: http://www.ninds.nih.gov/disorders/asperger/detail_asperger.htm#197423080.

Ogden, T.H. (1994). The analytic third: Working with intersubjective clinical facts. *International Journal of Psycho–analysis, 75,* 3–19.

Ogden, T. H. (1997). Some thoughts on the use of language in psychoanalysis. *Psychoanalytic Dialogues, 7,* 1–21.

Oppenheimer, R. (1956). Analogy in science. *American Psychologist, 11,* 127–135.

Owens, R.E. (2008). Development of pronouns. Excerpted from J.E. Owens, *Language Development: An Introduction.* NY: Allyn & Bacon. Retrieved from http://www.education.com/reference/article/development–pronouns–children.

Pally, R. (2001).A primary role for nonverbal communication in psychoanalysis. *Psychoanalytic Inquiry, 21,* 71–93.

Peller, L. (1966). Freud's contribution to language theory. *Psychoanalytic Study of the Child, 21,* 448–467.

Poirier, R. (1992). *Poetry and Pragmatism.* Cambridge, MA: Harvard University Press.

Rauch, S.L., Van der Kolk, B.A., Fisler, R.E., Alper, N.M., Orr, S.P., Savage C.R., et al. (1996). A symptom provocation study of posttraumatic stress disorder using positron emission tomography and script–driven imagery. *Archives of General Psychiatry, 53,* 380–387.

Rizzuto, A. (2002). Speech events, language development and the clinical situation. *International Journal of Psycho–Analysis, 83,* 1325–1343.

Rizzuto, A. (2003). Psychoanalysis: The transformation of the subject by the spoken word. *Psychoanalytic Quarterly, 72,* 287–323.

Rogers, A. G. (2006). *The Unsayable: The Hidden Language of Trauma.* NY: Ballantine Books.

Schiff–Meyers, N. (1993) Hearing Children of deaf parents. In D. Bishop & K. Mogford (Eds.), *Language Development in Exceptional Circumstances.* Hillsdale, NJ: Lawrence Erlbaum Associates. pp 47–61.

Shi, R., Werker, J.F. & Morgan J.L. (1999). Newborn infants' sensitivity to perceptual cues to lexical and grammatical words. *Cognition, 72,* B11–B21.

Sifneos, P. E. (1967).Clinical observations on some patients suffering from a variety of psychosomatic diseases. *ActaMedicinaPsychosomatica, 7,* 1–10.

Singh, L. (2008). Influences of high and low variability on infant word recognition. *Cognition, 106,* 833–870.

Skuse, D. H. (1984). Extreme deprivation in early childhood. I: Diverse outcomes for three siblings from an extraordinary family. *Journal of Child Psychology and Psychiatry, 25,* 523–541.

Skuse, D. H. (1993).Extreme deprivation in early childhood. In D. Bishop & K. Mogford (Eds.), *Language Development in Exceptional Circumstances.* Hillsdale, NJ: Lawrence Erlbaum Associates. pp. 29–46.

Spitz, R. A. (1965). *The First Year of Life.* New York: International Universities Press.

Stern, D. N. [Daniel]. (1985). *The Interpersonal World of the Infant.* NY: Basic Books.

Stern, D. N. [Daniel], Sander, L. S. W., Nahum, J. P., Harrison, A. M., Lyons–Ruth, K., Morgan, A. C., Bruschweilerstern, N., & Tronick, E. Z. (1998). Non–interpretive mechanisms in psychoanalytic therapy: The 'something more' than interpretation. *International Journal of Psycho–Analysis, 79,* 903–921.

Stern, D. B.[Donnel] (1987).Unformulated experience and transference. *Contemporary Psychoanalysis, 21,* 484–490.

Stern, D. B. [Donnell] (1997). *Unformulated Experience: From Dissociation to Imagination in Psychoanalysis.* Hillside, NJ: Analytic Press.

Stern, D. B. [Donnel] (2002). Words and wordlessness in the psychoanalytic situation. *Journal of the American Psychoanalytic Association, 50,* 221–247.

Stern, D. B. [Donnel] (2010). *Partners in Thought: Working with Unformulated Experience, Dissociation, and Enactment.* New York: Routledge. p. xv.

Stern, D. B. [Donnel] (2012). More meaning: Commentary on Vivona. *Journal of the American Psychoanalytic Association, 60,* 297–303.

Stolorow, R. & Atwood, R. (1992). *Contexts of Being: The Intersubjective Foundations of Psychological Life.* Hillside, NJ: Analytic Press.

Sullivan, H.S. (1947). *Conceptions of Modern Psychiatry.* Washington, DC: William Alanson White Psychiatric Foundation.

Tolpin, M. (1971). On the beginnings of a cohesive self—an application of the concept of transmuting internalization to the study of the transitional object and signal anxiety. *Psychoanalytic Study of the Child, 25,* 316–354.

Tomasello, M. & Rakoczy, H. (2003). What makes human cognition unique? From individual to shared to collective intentionality. *Mind & Language, 18,* 121–147.

Trevarthen, C. & Grant, F. (1979). Not work alone. *New Scientist, 81,* 566–569.

Vivona, J.M. (2003). Embracing figures of speech: The transformative potential of spoken language. *Psychoanalytic Psychology, 20,* 52–66.

Vivona, J.M. (2006). From developmental metaphor to developmental model: The shrinking role of language in the talking cure. *Journal of the American Psychoanalytic Association, 54,* 877–902.

Vivona, J.M. (2012). Is there a nonverbal period of development? *Journal of the American Psychoanalytic Association, 60,* 231–265.

Vouloumanos, A. & Werker, J.F. (2007). Listening to language at birth: Evidence for a bias for speech in neonates. *Developmental Science, 10,* 159–164.

Wallis, D., Musselman, C. & Mackay, S. (2004). Hearing mothers and their deaf children: The relationship between early, ongoing mode match and subsequent mental health functioning in adolescence. *Journal of Deaf Studies and Deaf Education, 9,* 2–14.

Wills, D.M. (1979). Early speech development in blind children, *Psychoanalytic Study of the Child, 34,* 85–117.

Wilson, A. & Weinstein, L. (1992). Language and the psychoanalytic process: Psychoanalysis and Vygotskian psychology, part II. *Journal of the American Psychoanalytic Association, 40,* 725–759.

Winnicott, D.W. (1960). The theory of the parent–infant relationship. *International Journal of Psycho–Analysis, 41,* 585–595.

Yoon, J.M.D., Johnson, M.H. & Csibra, G. (2008). Communication–induced memory biases in preverbal infants. *Proceedings of the National Academy of Sciences USA,* 105, 13690–13695.

Index

alexithymia, 78–79, 80. *See also* language development: inferences with
Amati-Mehler, 42–43, 46, 50
analogies, 103–104
Asperger's disorder. *See* language development: autistic spectrum disorder
autistic spectrum disorder, 77–78. *See also* language development: inferences with

blind children, 73–74. *See also* language development: interferences with
Broca's area, 84, 88

Chinese American Psychoanalytic Alliance (CAPA), 37, 39
clinical vignettes: Aaron, 32, 33, 38, 49; Barbara, 2, 33, 34–36, 109; Georgina, 80; Janet, 84–85, 88, 89, 93, 94, 99, 103; Joseph, 101; Lily, 31–32, 33, 38, 99, 108; Margaret, 92–93; Polly, 92, 93. *See also* Kay; Susan; Tom, 93
communicative third, 49

deaf children. *See* language development, interferences with, deaf children
developmental line of language acquisition. *See* language development
dissociative identity disorder, 90–91
dyadic nature of communication, 47

Edgcumbe, Rose, 54, 60, 62

emotional resonance of words, 43, 49, 68, 92, 97
Etezady, M. Hossein, vii, 39–40

feral children, 75–76. *See also* language development: inferences with
Fonagy, Peter, 61, 64, 112

Grandin, Temple, 77–78, 107

hearing child of deaf parents, 72. *See also* language development: interferences with
holding, 7, 58

jargon, 44–46

Kay, 2, 7–20, 50, 53, 79, 80, 95, 105, 107; collages, 19; colors, 8, 10, 11, 13, 14–15, 16, 16, 18–19; description of technique, 8, 11, 12, 16; painting, 8–16; Play Doh, 16–18; warrior woman, 11, 13, 14, 15, 16. *See also* clinical vignettes
Krapf, Eduardo, 31, 43

language: and emotions, 68, 93–94, 99; and fantasy, 65–66, 68, 102; and interpersonal "voice", 41, 42, 46–47, 64, 111; and lived experience, 50–51, 52, 93, 97–98; and meaning, 97–98, 99;

About the Author

Mary Davis, MD, is a Board Certified psychiatrist and child/adolescent psychiatrist, as well as a graduate psychoanalyst for both children and adults. She has been in practice since 1980, working in inpatient, outpatient, and residential treatment settings. She has been interested in the ways language facilitates and interferes with our social functioning since her days in training.